# Praise for *Plain*

"A deeply honest, forthright, and forgiving account of finding one's way as a gay Mennonite. *Plain* shows how we the misplaced faithful take the truths of our upbringing to create beautiful stories, homes, and lives."—Joanna Brooks, author of *The Book of Mormon Girl*

"A wise and wonderful memoir about breaking away from tradition, then finally discovering its value. This clear-eyed yet affectionate coming-of-age story will resonate with anyone who has ever struggled to separate from their family and find their true, authentic self."
—Sharon Harrigan, author of *Playing with Dynamite*

"Filled with a familiar equanimity, grace, and droll humor. This book is as simple and nourishing as fresh vegetable soup and as complex as a Tibetan mandala. It will leave you pondering the depth of a single word: plain."—Shirley Showalter, author of *Blush: A Mennonite Girl Meets a Glittering World*

"While *Plain* is a quiet memoir, it's not a slow read. Mary Alice uses humor, yearnings, and curiosity to build dramatic tension within the mundane experiences of farm life. . . . The care she uses to develop this world in early chapters gave me a deep appreciation for the culture in which she grew up and deep empathy for the longings she faced within this world that served her yet didn't fully see her. . . . Not all rebellions need to be loud and in your face. Sometimes the quieter ones have the greatest power."—*Hippocampus Magazine*

"[A] powerful memoir. . . . Very highly recommended."
—*Midwest Book Review*

# Living Out

Gay and Lesbian Autobiographies

David Bergman, Joan Larkin, and Raphael Kadushin,
*Founding Editors*

# PLAIN

## A Memoir of
## Mennonite Girlhood

Mary Alice Hostetter

THE UNIVERSITY OF WISCONSIN PRESS

Publication of this book has been made possible, in part,
through support from the Anonymous Fund of the College of
Letters and Science at the University of Wisconsin–Madison.

The University of Wisconsin Press
728 State Street, Suite 443
Madison, Wisconsin 53706
uwpress.wisc.edu

Printed in Canada
This book may be available in a digital edition.

Library of Congress Cataloging-in-Publication Data

Names: Hostetter, Mary Alice, author.
Title: Plain : a memoir of Mennonite girlhood / Mary Alice Hostetter.
Other titles: Living out.
Description: Madison, Wisconsin : The University of Wisconsin Press, [2022]
| Series: Living out: gay and lesbian autobiographies
Identifiers: LCCN 2022022536 | ISBN 9780299340407 (hardcover)
Subjects: LCSH: Hostetter, Mary Alice. | Mennonites—Pennsylvania—
Lancaster County—Biography.
Classification: LCC BX8143.H67 A3 2022 | DDC 289.7/74815—dc23/eng/20220701
LC record available at https://lccn.loc.gov/2022022536

ISBN 9780299340445 (pbk.)

Some names of people and places have been changed.

To my brothers and sisters,
who shared in this journey,
all in their own way.

*and*

To Terry,
for being there for me
at every stage of this book's
creation.

# Contents

# PROLOGUE

# Girl at the Market

A Mennonite girl at the outdoor farmers' market in Charlottesville weighs vegetables for the man in front of me. She places bag after bag on the scales—potatoes, tomatoes, green beans. Careful and unhurried with each one, she waits for the scale to stop quivering so the weight is accurate. She appears to be a teenager and wears a simple long dress and a prayer covering perched on hair pulled back into tight braids. I'm surprised they're still using straight pins to hold their prayer coverings in place, but what else would they use? Something needs to keep them from blowing away. How I always wished mine would blow away, but it wouldn't have mattered. There were always more at the covering store where my mother took me.

The girl is friendly, but in a reserved, studied kind of way, as if she would never want to appear too forward. She smiles as she hands the man change from the twenty he's given her, and he doesn't look at it before shoving it in his pocket and moving on, no doubt certain a young Mennonite girl would never cheat a customer. He's probably right. I can't imagine it either.

I hand her my tomatoes and eggplant, and she weighs them. I look at her. How can I not? I *am* her, or at least I once was. Surely she's self-conscious about her clothing and wishing she were somewhere else on this hot Saturday morning. When she looks at the women shopping, she must wonder if any of them have daughters her age and what they might be doing. The woman on her cell phone could be talking to her

daughter, who might be asking if she can go to the swimming pool
with her friends this afternoon, or to a movie later. The Mennonite girl
must wish for that life. When she watches the middle-aged woman
choosing green beans one by one and dropping them into her bag, she
may remember helping her mother pick those beans the evening before.
In the failing light, she and her mother grabbed them by the handfuls
and dropped them into the baskets. As the sun set, they couldn't even
see what they were picking, just feeling for them. Maybe that's why
there were leaves here and there among the beans.

"You can tell these beans are fresh," the woman says to another, picking a leaf out from among the beans and dropping it on the ground.

Can the Mennonite girl tell I was once like her? Can she see, even
though I'm wearing shorts and a sleeveless top on this warm summer
morning, that the tan lines from my first eighteen years of life stopped
at my elbows and knees from dressing in modest clothes while I worked
in the sun? Like hers, no doubt. Although my hair, with out-of-control
curls in the dog-day humidity, has not been pulled back into tight braids
or a bun in years, can she tell from my hairline that for so many years it
had been? Do I have a look that, even now, she might be able to detect?

If I had become who I was expected to be, that Mennonite girl might
have been my daughter or granddaughter, but I look at her as if she is
my young self. I'm sure it never occurs to her to feel any kinship with
me. I'm just another woman shopping at the market.

It wasn't so long ago that the Mennonite Church split after a bitter
conflict over gay inclusion in leadership and membership. I wonder
how she feels about the issue dividing her church. I'm sure she's heard
sermons on the topic, no doubt condemning the sin of homosexuality.
Does she pay any attention? I never remember it being mentioned from
the pulpit when I was a teenager, but I doubt I would have paid attention either. It would have seemed one of those odd things preachers
mentioned now and then, things like the prohibition on swearing oaths
or joining lodges, things that had nothing to do with me.

What if I asked her about what was going on with her church? "So
how do you feel about the Mennonite Church splitting over the gay
issue?" I might say.

"I don't even think about it," she might respond.

"But don't the preachers talk about it? Seems like a big thing if it split the whole church."

"I'm sure they talk about it, but I don't pay much attention. We're in the country, so we don't have any of those people in our church," she might say. "That's more of a city problem."

What if I told her I was once in the country too and didn't pay much attention to my Mennonite preachers either? When I was a teenager, I might have said the words I imagine coming from her mouth.

I wonder what she'd think if I told her about my marriage to a woman, who is even now a few stalls down at the market buying sunflowers. The wedding was on a beautiful spring day in one of the gardens at the University of Virginia. Both of our families were there to support us and bear witness. Most of them had never attended such an event. Some of them could never have imagined it, but they were there for us that day.

Most of my eleven siblings, some of whom I'd never felt comfortable sharing that part of my life with, were there, along with nieces and nephews, friends, my wife's two children. The retired juvenile court judge my wife and I had worked with in our professional lives said she was honored when we asked her to officiate for us. She read Supreme Court Justice Anthony Kennedy's majority opinion in the case that legalized same-sex marriage. "In forming a marital union," he wrote, "two people become something greater than they once were."

A nephew read a selection from *The Velveteen Rabbit*: "Generally, by the time you are Real, most of your hair has been loved off, and your eyes drop out and you get loose in your joints and very shabby. But these things don't matter at all, because once you are Real, you can't be ugly, except to people who don't understand." It seemed an appropriate reading for two almost seventy-year-old brides.

I read my wife a Mary Oliver poem, "I Have Just Said," and she read me one from Emily Dickinson, "It's All I Have to Bring Today," before we said our vows.

Our son-in-law, a musician, played "Love at Home" on his saxophone. It was a Mennonite hymn that had become a family anthem. As a jazz musician, it was not part of his regular repertoire, so he'd spent time learning it.

I should tell the girl about the beautiful wooden cupcake stand one of my brothers made, carefully turning on his lathe the delicate spindles to separate the layers. One of my sisters and a niece made the miniature cupcakes to put on the stand for the reception. I don't know what she'd make of it if I told her we had an artist friend painting the scene from an unobtrusive corner of the garden.

I want the Mennonite girl to pay attention to what is happening in her church, perhaps because I fear I would not have done so if the controversy had happened when I was her age. I'd like her to know that the battle over gay and lesbian rights affects real people and divides real families. It isn't just a city problem.

I don't know how she would react if I were to tell her about the wedding. When I was a teenager, I'm sure I would have been incredulous that such a thing could happen, maybe even a bit horrified. I imagine giving her a card with my phone number, in case she wants to talk about how I got away, but why do I assume she wants a blueprint for escape? There is a certain arrogance in the very thought. She looks content, healthy. I have no reason to believe she feels embarrassed or trapped. She may want nothing more than to grow up to have a life like her mother's. Did I once feel that way? Ever?

She glances toward her father, who asks if she needs more green beans from the van. She smiles at her younger brothers, who toss peppers at each other, and I remember playing with my brothers and sisters like that when we worked in the field and garden. Neither the girl nor her brothers seem to be unhappy with who they are or where they are or what they're doing.

Looking at the Mennonite girl, I want to understand how I found my way from a world that might have been similar to hers to where I am now. What were the signposts, and who were my guides? Where were the forks in the road? There must have been crossroads and paths not taken; however, my journey seems a gentle unfolding of inevitability. In some ways it seems I have gone a long distance, in other ways, not far at all.

# PART ONE

Family photo, circa 1951. *Back row, left to right*: Jim, Ike, Milt; *middle row*: Ray, Charles, Rhoda, Abe; *front row*: Mary Alice, Nancy, Mother, Grace, Daddy, Sanford, Dale.

# Hot Lard

The three of us sat on the bench beside the long kitchen table, which was stretched as far as it would go. There were twelve of us in the family, plus my parents. Although some of my older brothers and sisters had already left home, they still needed a place at the table when they came back to visit with their husbands, wives, and children. I was seven years old, and I sat on the end of the bench nearest the stove . . . but not too near. The bench was just the right size for three of us. My brother Sanford was five, and he sat at the other end; my little sister, Nancy, between us. She was only three, and my mother said we should make sure she didn't get down off the bench. She didn't even try.

"Stay there," Mother said, "until I'm finished with the doughnuts. Lard is almost hot."

I knew about hot lard. I'd heard the story about Katie Lapp so many times, I could have told it myself. Katie was an Amish neighbor. I could imagine her apron strings catching on the handle of an iron skillet, and the whole pan of grease spilling down the backs of her legs. Watching Mother working by the stove, it was easy to see how it could happen, but she was careful, turning the handle of the skillet to the back where her apron strings wouldn't catch on it, moving carefully whenever she went near the stove. I knew she would be safe.

"Poor Katie was burned so bad," Mother had said, "for a while she could hardly walk. Doctors didn't know if her legs would ever heal. And she was in such pain. There's nothing like pain from a burn."

When I saw Katie, she seemed to walk all right.

"Those burn scars on her legs are just awful," my mother said. But Katie always wore long dresses, so I never saw her scars. I don't know how Mother did.

She had other stories too, my mother. There was the one about our cousin, who broke off part of his front tooth when he was playing around in the bathtub with his brother. Mother told us that story when we were in the tub for our Saturday bath, Sanford, Nancy, and I—the little ones in the family—and she wanted us to understand why we shouldn't play around. I could have told you about our neighbor's Fresh Air boy who came from New York City as part of a program to give city kids a chance to spend a couple of weeks on the farm in the summer. He fell down the hay hole in the loft, even though he was told to stay away from it. He broke his arm and had to go back to New York on the train wearing a cast and a sling.

It never occurred to me to doubt Mother's stories. Even now, years later, I am certain they were true, certain there were chipped teeth and broken bones and scarred legs, the cost of carelessness or disobedience.

Earlier, before Mother had dropped dollops of lard into the largest black skillet and put it on the stove, I had helped her cut out the doughnuts. She made the big circles with the round cookie cutter, and I made the hole in the middle. I used the little olive jar, dipping it in the flour before pushing it down on the soft dough, all the way through. Then I tapped the hole out of the olive jar and put it on the tablecloth to rise, right next to the doughnuts. I got the holes in the center and remembered to dip the olive jar in the flour every time to keep the holes from sticking.

Sanford thought he was old enough to help with the doughnuts, but he wasn't. He was only five. I didn't think he could remember to dip the olive jar in the flour every time, and he wouldn't know where the middle of the circle was. I'm sure he would have tried to eat the dough, and you couldn't do that. Besides, he was a boy, and what boys did in the kitchen was come to the table to eat what women and girls had prepared for them.

The doughnuts and the holes were already puffing up, and Mother was cutting open brown paper bags and spreading them on the yellow Formica countertop to blot the grease when the doughnuts were finished frying. It was magic the way the doughnuts puffed up all by themselves. Mother said it was the yeast that caused it.

The kitchen smelled of yeast and hot lard, but I could still smell my father's and brothers' coveralls and coats, even though they had put on their barn clothes and gone out to clean the stables and feed and milk the cows a while before. Their clothes smelled like hay and feed, and a little of manure.

Mother rinsed the bowl and wooden spoon she'd used to mix the dough. Behind her, through the windows, I could see it was still snowing, big fluffy flakes drifting down to the garden, which was already white. Around the inside of the two windows hung the sweet potato vine my mother planted in the hanging pot the fall before. She'd put in tacks and string to train the vine around the windows. It had grown so long, it went across the top and down the sides, almost all the way to the floor. How could all those leaves and vines come from a single sweet potato?

She put the bowl and spoon in the drainer and dried her hands on her apron. "Time for the test," she said, and picked up one of the doughnut holes and dropped it into the hot grease.

From the bench I could hear the quick sizzle and see the hole dip under and back to the top, moving gently in the hot lard. When the doughnut hole was golden brown, Mother took it out with a slotted spoon and put it on the paper.

"Looks like the lard is good and hot," she said.

We sat and watched as she dropped in the doughnut holes, one after the other. They bobbed in the hot grease, like little ducks. When she had dipped out all the holes, she put in the big doughnuts, flipping them with the long-handled fork. I liked to watch her. She did it so fast, and the hot lard didn't splash at all.

On the bench we sat and waited.

I don't know if the kitchen was as big as I remember it, but at the time it felt huge. That warm kitchen, especially in winter, was our world. It was dominated by the table, chairs, and bench, and, of course, the cook stove. In the corner by the telephone was my father's rocking chair, and, at the end of the kitchen, the sideboard, a massive cupboard, where we stacked our schoolbooks. Tucked in beside the refrigerator was the high chair. Even though none of us needed a high chair anymore, there were always nieces and nephews visiting.

I remember the kitchen as clean. There were never dishes stacked by the sink; we dried them and put them away after every meal. In the wintertime, it was the most comfortably warm room in the house, so the kitchen table is where we did schoolwork, played board games, or read. On Saturday evening we gathered around the table to study the lesson for the Mennonite Sunday school we attended every week. Even if the linoleum was worn, it was clean. Mother scrubbed the floor on her hands and knees. She said it was the only right way to clean a floor, insisting a mop simply smeared the dirt around.

When Mother had finished frying all the doughnuts, she took a plate from the cupboard. She put nine of the doughnut holes on it, sprinkled them with powdered sugar, and set them on the table in front of us.

"Here you are," she said.

I never considered the doughnuts being about anything but an occasional treat, but they may have been. In a family where I never heard either of my parents say "I love you" in their ninety-plus years, I also never felt unloved, perhaps because treats like doughnuts were as clear an expression of love as hearing the words. At least that's how it felt to me.

And the doughnuts provided another lesson too. Listen to your mother, and stay in your place. One of the first Bible verses we learned in Mennonite Sunday school was "Children, obey your parents." If I listened to my mother, I had no doubt I'd be safe . . . and get sweet, warm doughnut holes.

When I was seven, I was innocent, not yet worried about heaven and hell. I did not know then there would come a time when I was tormented by the notion of hellfire and painful burning, not quite believing it, but not disbelieving either. The only sin I gave much thought was disobeying my parents. I saw no reason not to stay in my place, just as Mother asked. With all those older brothers and sisters, she had to know there would come a time when I would no longer want to stay on the bench, that there might be a time I would not want to do what was expected of me. I didn't yet know that. Back then, all I wanted was to be a good girl.

# Class Pictures

Even before my accident, I was a bit nervous about second grade. School would begin in a few weeks, and my older brothers Ray and Dale started telling me scary stories. They were sitting at the kitchen table playing Figmill. I watched as they took turns pushing black and white buttons from Mother's button box around on lines drawn on a piece of cardboard.

While Ray thought about his next move, Dale looked up at me. "Boy, you're in trouble. You'll have Miss Brock this year."

She had started teaching at our elementary school the year before, and I'd be the first in our family to be in her class.

"What's wrong with Miss Brock?"

"Last school she taught at, she killed a kid."

"More than one," Ray said.

"Now stop with that nonsense," Mother said, lining up canning jars on the counter.

"How did she do it?" I asked.

"She smacked him on the head a little too hard and hit the spot that can kill you with a single whack," Dale said.

"There was the other kid too," Ray said, "the one she shoved down the stairs. Broke his neck, and she said it was an accident. But it was her fault."

"Didn't she get in trouble?" I said.

"People never knew. She was sneaky about it," Ray said.

"You better be careful, is all I'm saying." Dale pushed a white button into position to make a row. "Figmill."

Mother kept a scrapbook of newspaper clippings about important events—farm accidents, murders, kidnappings, traffic accidents, weddings of neighbors or relatives. With all the articles she'd cut out, I was sure a story about a teacher killing kids, or kids dying for no reason, would be included in her scrapbook. I looked at her scrapbook often, and I hadn't seen a thing about it. We got the Lancaster *Intelligencer Journal* every day but Sunday, and it had news about all sorts of things. I could read a lot of the words myself, and I knew school kids dying was more important than a lot of stories in the newspaper.

I loved school. In first grade I had learned to read books about Dick and Jane and Sally. The stories weren't very interesting, because those kids didn't do much—jump, run, look, go—and there were only three of them. But I liked learning to read new words. I loved the idea that the alphabet letters tacked up over the blackboard could turn into words, and words could turn into stories. Imagine. I knew I would learn more words in second grade and read new stories. Even with a nagging concern about Miss Brock, I mostly looked forward to second grade.

On the first day, I waited for the school bus with Ray and Dale. Ray was in sixth grade and Dale in fourth. I clutched my new pencil box, with three freshly sharpened pencils, a six-inch ruler, a big eraser, and a protractor. I didn't know what it was for, but if I drew around it twice, I could almost make a circle, color it, and turn it into a sun. In the little drawer at the bottom of the pencil box was a tiny notepad and a box with six crayons, which was a start, but it really wasn't enough colors.

Mrs. Robinson, my first-grade teacher, had been sweet and seemed soft. She was always happy and made me feel good. I thought all teachers would be like that. She chose me to read a poem in front of the whole PTA. I had to memorize it and stand up to recite it for the grownups at their meeting one evening. I was happy she had picked me.

I like to dry the dishes,
Because it's helping Mother,

And it's such a pleasant time
To talk to one another.

I remembered every word, and Mother said I did a great job; she said
everyone could hear me and I had good expression. I wasn't sure what
she meant, but I felt proud anyway. The next day at school, although
the other kids hadn't heard me recite my poem, it seemed they somehow knew how well I had done, the way they looked at me. Maybe
their parents told them about it when they got home from the meeting.

I could tell as soon as I saw Miss Brock that she was not going to be
like Mrs. Robinson. Miss Brock was tall and thin, all hard, sharp angles,
nothing soft about her. She seldom smiled and she spoke in a snippy
little voice that made you feel you had done something to make her
angry, even if she was asking you to open your reading book . . . and
you did it right away. On the first day, I looked at her and remembered
what Ray and Dale had told me. I imagined what she might be capable
of and knew I would do whatever I could not to cross her. I had a way
of not making trouble in school. Ever. If anyone in my second-grade
class was in danger from Miss Brock, I was certain it wouldn't be me,
because I was a good girl.

The beginning of the school year was uneventful and fun. I liked seeing friends I hadn't seen all summer. We played on the swings and see-
saw at recess; we read chapter books and learned to multiply. As far as
I could tell, Miss Brock was not hurting anyone. Ray and Dale got tired
of reminding me how dangerous she was, only occasionally saying something like "She kill anyone yet?" I knew who they were talking about.

Only a few weeks after school started, the stories about Bobby
Greenlease's kidnapping and murder made the *Intelligencer Journal*. Even
though it happened far away, in Missouri, people were talking about it
and writing about it in our newspaper. The paper printed what looked
like Bobby's school picture on the front page, and he looked like the
boys in my class, smiling at the camera. I thought about Bobby Greenlease a lot, and it made me sad and a little afraid. I couldn't imagine how
a kid nearly my age would be kidnapped and murdered, even though

his parents paid all that money to get him back. It bothered me. Mother said we'd be all right, because children were kidnapped only if their parents were rich, and we were not. When she told me that, it made me feel lucky in a way, but still . . . He was six years old, kidnapped and shot dead, buried in the yard of the woman who'd come to pick him up at school. She told the school people Bobby's mother was sick and asked her to pick him up. I knew I'd never leave school with someone I'd never seen before, not like he did, but the whole thing worried me anyway, knowing kids could be killed like that. It didn't make me feel better, Mother saying Bobby was safe in Jesus's arms now. Nothing against Jesus, but it seemed to me Bobby'd just as soon keep on being a kid for a while longer.

The day my accident happened, a couple months into the school year, I asked Miss Brock if I could go to the girls' room. She said I could wait until lunchtime, but I couldn't. Why would I have said I needed to go if I didn't? I tried to hold it, but a trickle became a puddle, and the puddle became an embarrassing stream, flowing up the row, under Hayes's desk in front of me, all the way to Tommy's desk in front of him.

Hayes raised his hand. "We have an accident here." His voice was louder than it needed to be, and he made a scene, pulling his feet up on his desk, as if a rushing river of pee would wash him away. Miss Brock walked back toward me and looked under my desk. "Let's go back to the cloak room." I followed her, looking at the floor as if it would keep everyone from being able to see me, and she asked me to take off my underpants. The way she said it made me afraid, and I didn't consider not doing what she told me.

"Put them on the radiator. They'll dry quicker," she said. She looked and sounded mad, the way she pointed and shook her finger at me, as if I had wet my pants on purpose. She grabbed a worn towel from the closet and shoved it at me. "Here, you can sit on that. Now go on back to your desk."

In that moment I was sure she could kill children, and I almost wished I was the kid she smacked on the head a little too hard, finding the perfect spot that could kill you in a single whack. But she didn't smack me, and I had to slink back to my desk, stopping at the radiator to hang up my sopping underpants. My wet slip and dress clung to the backs of my legs. My drooping brown stockings were wet, as were the elastic garters that were supposed to hold them up. I was sure everyone was staring at me, knowing I was not wearing underwear. I sat down on the worn towel. And there my underpants hung, draped over the hissing, wheezing radiator. Miss Brock spread another worn towel under my desk to soak up the puddle.

Hayes turned around in his desk and smiled. I thought he was laughing at me, which wasn't fair. In first grade, when we were doing our art projects, Hayes was working next to me and vomited all over my papier-mâché giraffe. I had let Mrs. Robinson know about the vomit, but I spoke in a quiet voice, and I didn't laugh at him. He ruined my art project, which had taken a long time as I dipped strip after strip of torn paper in glue and smoothed it onto my giraffe. It looked beautiful, with its yellow paint and brown spots. Hayes didn't get any vomit on his own project, which he said was a turtle with its feet and head pulled inside its shell. It looked like a brown rock, and it would have been no great loss to art if he had vomited on his turtle, but he had to turn his head and ruin my giraffe. It smelled like vomit after that, and I didn't want to take it home. I hated to throw it away after I had worked so hard on it, but what could I do? Mother never got to see it.

When lunch time came, Miss Brock must have knocked on the door to the boiler room, where Mr. Hershey, the janitor, had his office, and asked him to come take care of things with his mop and wheely bucket, like he had after Hayes's vomit accident. There was no need for Miss Brock to tell him who caused the accident, but she may have anyway. I saw Mr. Hershey in the hallway when the class was walking back from the lunchroom, and the way he looked at me made me feel like he may have known it was me. By the time we got back to our classroom after lunch, the floor was clean, the worn towels taken away. I could smell the cleaner Mr. Hershey used on the floor. It smelled like pine trees and was so strong it made my eyes and nose burn.

After all the other kids had gone outside for afternoon recess, Miss Brock said my underpants were probably dry enough to put back on, and I did. The dry panties felt stiff, but I was glad to have them back where they belonged and not hanging where everyone in the class could see them. When I got home from school, I told Mother about the accident. "I'll try to remember to make sure you go to the bathroom before you leave for school," she said, and told me to take off my dirty clothes and put them in the laundry basket. She wasn't angry at all, not like Miss Brock.

For a while after the accident, I woke up each day not feeling well and told Mother I was too sick to go to school. It felt to me I could only be safe if I stayed at home with her.

"What hurts?" she asked.

"It's a bellyache," I said.

After the bus disappeared down the highway, and all the big boys had gone to school, I came downstairs and said I felt better. I was ready to play with Nancy and Sanford, who were too little for school. After a few days of bellyaches, Mother said I needed to stay in bed if I was too sick to go to school, and *that* wasn't any fun at all.

When I look back on that time, I realize she didn't make me drink boneset tea or take a spoonful of castor oil. She didn't lather my chest with blue grease. It was almost as if she knew my illness would not respond to the usual remedies. Some days, if I told her I was feeling better, she'd have my father—Daddy, we all called him, even my mother—drop me off at school when he took the milk to the creamery in town. Going in late embarrassed me more than going in on time.

School was what children were expected to do and what I wanted to do. It didn't take long—maybe days or a couple weeks—before the pull to return to school was stronger than the bellyaches. I missed seeing the other kids, playing outside at recess, learning new things, even if it was from Miss Brock. Soon I was going to school on time every day, as I had in first grade. We got started learning division and read harder books. Some days I didn't think about how awful it had been the day my underpants were draped on the radiator under the windows, and I didn't worry about Miss Brock smacking someone on the head, on the spot that could kill you right away. All that mattered was being in school; it's where I wanted to be.

I know we received report cards, and there must have been a class picture. Although I have them for all my other years of school, I can't find anything for second grade. I'd like to see if Miss Brock smiled for the picture, whether Hayes looked mean or kind, whether I looked happy to be in school.

I am, no doubt, the only one in that second-grade class who remembers the day Miss Brock asked me to hang my panties on the radiator. I did not think I could ever show my face in that class again, but somehow I did. Showing up again was an extra lesson I learned that year. I am not grateful to Miss Brock for what she did, but, when I look back on that time, I am grateful for my mother's gentle wisdom in patiently allowing me to recover from my mysterious "illness," then nudging me to do what she knew I wanted and needed to do.

We didn't memorize any poetry in second grade—maybe Miss Brock didn't like poetry—but we got back to it in third grade when I learned to recite "The Swing," all three verses, with the second stanza I loved:

Up in the air and over the wall,
   Till I can see so wide,
Rivers and trees and cattle and all,
   Over the countryside.

Neither my third-grade teacher nor I could have known then how important words would become for me or how single-minded I would become in seeking broader vistas.

# Once Upon a Time

Mother wet the tips of her fingers in a pan of water and shook them to sprinkle the drops over the dry laundry spread on the kitchen table. Why go to all the trouble to hang it on the clothesline until it was dry, I wondered, and then wet it again?

"It makes it easier to iron," she said.

After dipping the collars and cuffs of the white shirts in the starch she had boiled and cooled, she rolled up all the damp laundry—shirts, pants, aprons, hankies, blouses—in a pile and ironed her way through, piece by piece.

If Sanford, Nancy, and I sat on the bench while she ironed, Mother told us stories. Even after I could read my own stories, I liked to listen to hers. She told us the one about the careless boy who forgot to turn off the bathtub faucet, and the tub overflowed, water pouring through the ceiling of the dining room and onto his birthday cake. It ruined his party. She told the one about the flood and the children who floated out the window in a bathtub to escape to safety. I never thought to wonder why she liked flood stories so much. And she told us the one about the schoolchildren and the precipice. It was one of my favorites.

"This one is mostly true," Mother said.

I leaned forward on the bench.

"Once upon a time," she said, the hot iron hissing on the collar of Daddy's Sunday shirt, "a long time ago, out West somewhere, school-children got up one winter morning, and it was warm as spring. Some

of them didn't wear hats or gloves or coats to school, because it was
that warm. They played outside at recess and lunchtime. Sometime in
the afternoon, a cold wind started blowing, and the snow came down,
and the teachers told the children to go home early, before it got worse.
It got worse quickly, and many of them couldn't tell which way to walk,
whether they were going toward home or not. Everything was white,
and the snow blew sideways. Parents went out looking for their children, and some of them got lost. They were calling out to each other,
but the wind was howling, and many of the children couldn't hear their
parents."

Mother put the white shirt on a hanger and hung it from the rack on
the dining room door, buttoning the top button. She spread out a damp
handkerchief and started ironing it.

"At one school the teacher kept two children back, because they
were little, and their farm was a long way off. She lived near the school
and told them they could wait at her house until the storm died down.
The wind was blowing so hard, she could hardly open the schoolhouse
door. She told them to hold her hands. None of them, not even the
teacher, could see her house through the blowing snow. She tried to
wrap her coat around them as they started walking. The little girl began
to cry and said she was cold. The teacher told them they were almost
to her house, but still she couldn't see anything but white—no road,
no fences, not even a tree. The cold cut through her coat. The teacher
knew about a precipice not far from her house, where the land dropped
away. She didn't want to take them toward the precipice, but she didn't
know which way she was going."

I had never heard the word "precipice" before my mother told that
story, and I liked it, the way it hissed with danger.

"They never found the teacher's house," Mother said. "They were
lost."

"But lost isn't the same as dead, is it?" Sanford asked.

"Sometimes it can be."

I knew in this story lost and dead *were* the same. One time when
Sanford and Nancy weren't around, I had asked Mother how it really
happened, and she told me.

"Well," she had said, "they didn't stay lost. Months later, when the snow melted, one of the neighbors found them in a field in the opposite direction from the teacher's house, not far from the precipice. They were covered by the teacher's coat, and she was still holding their hands, but they were dead."

Sometimes, after she finished telling the story, Mother added, "You just never know," almost like she was talking to herself. Back then I didn't know what she meant, but I grew to understand she was probably saying you never know when your time will come, and it might be you frozen in the snow, or when the Lord might return to collect the faithful and take them to heaven. You needed to be ready. And I was sure that I was.

I liked the story, but I thought the ending could have been better. Why couldn't there be a miracle? The parents must have been praying. Why couldn't Mother have told the story with the children being rescued, like in the Bible story about Daniel in the Lion's Den? He was trapped in the den with the dangerous lions all night, and when they opened the den the next morning, they found the lions had not touched him. There were lots of miracles in the stories my mother read to us at bedtime from *Egermeier's Bible Story Book*. In one of them, Lazarus was dead and came back to life; in another, there was enough bread and fish to feed thousands, with only seven loaves and a few fish to start with. I knew things could happen, even when it didn't look good. We'd seen the stories played out on the flannel board at our Mennonite Sunday school when the minister's wife called all the children up front for the Children's Meetings before the sermon.

I didn't think much about it then, but many of the Bible stories we heard were violent, and one of the central beliefs of our church was pacifism and nonviolence. I'm not sure what children were to make of all that Old Testament slaying: David killing Goliath with a well-aimed stone from his slingshot; Samson pulling down an entire building and crushing the people gathered there; Daniel's captors being thrown into the lions' den, where they were instantly killed. The stories had a lot of violence and not much turning-the-other-cheek, which is what we were supposed to do.

In Mother's story, having the teacher and the schoolchildren find their way in the blizzard would be an easy change to make. They could have heard their parents calling for them during a break in the storm. As Mother's story went, the teacher was trying to keep the children safe, and the children were doing what the grownup asked them to do. There was no reason for the story to turn out so badly. That's the thing with stories—you can make them turn out however you want.

If I told the story, I'd tell it right. The snow would stop long enough for the teacher and schoolchildren to figure out where they were and find their way to a nearby house, where they'd warm up next to a blazing fire and eat the soup the farmer's wife had made. They could eat cookies and drink hot chocolate. The snow wouldn't start up again until everyone was safely back with their families. That's how the story should have gone. But then it wouldn't be true.

It didn't bother me having the precipice in the story. I'd keep the precipice, as long as the children found their way home. Every story needs something like a precipice, some danger just out of sight, as long as I knew I was safe.

"Can you tell us the story about the time Ray got into the beehives?" Sanford said when Mother had finished the precipice story.

"All right," Mother said, "this is how it happened. I took Ray along when I went out to pick strawberries up by the orchard. He was just a little thing, but he could walk and got into everything. I needed strawberries for shortcake. He wasn't out of my sight for a minute when I saw him up by the beehives in the orchard. I called for him to stop, but he went right on."

She folded the tablecloth in half so she could drape it over the ironing board.

"I got under that fence so fast and ran to catch up, but, by the time I got to him, bees were swarming all over. I grabbed him and ran toward the house. They were stinging me, too, but I didn't care. He went limp while I carried him, flimsy as a ragdoll. I laid him down on the sofa and called the doctor. He said to keep him still and cool and get out as many stingers as I could. By the time the doctor got here, Ray had woken up but still acted real sleepy, crying a little. I'll tell you, I was never so happy to hear a child cry as I was that day."

She folded the tablecloth a couple more times until it was small enough to fit in the tablecloth drawer. She picked up a damp handkerchief. "The doctor said I should keep an eye on him and let him know if he started running a fever or vomiting. For days after that, I was sure he smelled like honey."

"He should have listened," I said, "and not gone near the hives."

"He was too little to know better," Mother said. "Maybe he didn't even hear me."

"Could he have died?" Sanford said. "Was it a miracle?"

"I'm just glad it turned out the way it did."

Mother ironed the last handkerchief, folded it, and added it to the pile.

Soon I'd be old enough to help with the ironing. I'd start with red hankies, then white ones. I'd be allowed to iron aprons and barn pants, flannel shirts. Mother would sometimes ask me to sprinkle the laundry and roll it up. I'd never get to iron my father's and brothers' white shirts with starched cuffs and collars. Only Mother did those.

As I got older I would hear more true stories about neighbors and relatives, people we didn't even know. Some of the stories turned out right, and some of them did not. Not all of them made the newspaper or my mother's scrapbook. Even with the occasional bad stories, most things in my world felt predictable, safe, and calm. In other places, some far away or not so far away from our farm on the hill, there was danger and excitement, but it seemed we were out of harm's way.

# Making Soup

I was ten years old, and I'd helped my mother make vegetable soup lots of times, picking and peeling, shelling and husking, digging and chopping. I knew what went into vegetable soup. I'd helped plant the seeds from the time I was so short I scarcely needed to bend over to drop them into the soft dirt.

"You're down where you need to be," Mother would say, showing Sanford and Nancy and me how far apart to scatter the seeds in the trench she'd dug in the garden with the corner of her hoe. She tapped stakes in at either end of the row and stretched the baler twine tight between them as a guide. She liked her rows straight.

I knew what the seeds looked and felt like: the smooth, dark, speckled bean seeds, the shriveled corn seeds, carrot seeds so small they could blow away. I never thought about it being a miracle, the way little dried-up seeds could turn into crops that turned into food. It was the way it worked. And I knew about the vegetables when they were grown too. I could tell when the lima beans were full enough to pick, or when the sweet corn was ready, the tassel on top of the cobs dry and brown. I had helped Mother make soup, doing my part, but I'd never done it by myself.

When I came down the back stairs that morning, the kitchen still smelled faintly of frying bacon from the breakfast Mother had made for my father and brothers. I had gotten up too late for that breakfast— bacon and eggs, fried potatoes, and toast. She was rinsing the last of the suds down the drain in the sink. The summer sun streamed in the window behind her.

"I'm taking Aunt Mabel to New Holland, and Nancy and Sanford are going along to get shoes," she said. "While we're gone, I'd like you to make vegetable soup."

"By myself?"

"You think you can do it?"

"Sure," I said.

"You know where things are, either the field or the garden. I've put the soup bones on to simmer. Don't change the burner." She adjusted the knob, making the flame so low I could hardly see it. "The soup bones can cook while you're out in the field. Dip them out when you're ready to add the vegetables. Fill the whole pot."

I was surprised she trusted me to make soup. Sure, I could make Tiptop Cake from the *Mennonite Community Cookbook*, but that was different. All I had to do was follow the directions. And cake was dessert. But soup was a responsibility. Soup was for supper, and my father and brothers would be hungry after working in the fields and barn all day. Of course, we'd be hungry too, Mother, Nancy, and I, but for some reason, men's hunger always seemed to be bigger, or count for more. I never thought to question that.

I finished eating my corn flakes and rinsed the bowl. After Mother took off her apron and hung it on the hook by the door, she and Sanford and Nancy got in the black Buick and drove down the lane. It would have been fun to go along to New Holland to shop at Rubinson's Store. Mother had said Aunt Mabel needed to shop for a dress. I knew she wasn't buying a real dress, only a piece of fabric to make a dress. Mother said she'd make me a few new dresses for school, and I could help choose the fabric. The pieces on the remnant table at Rubinson's were often big enough, so we always looked for remnants first. But there would be time for choosing dresses later, and they all looked pretty much the same anyway, the same pattern. That day I was making soup.

Mother left before I could ask her to remind me of all the things that went into vegetable soup. I should have asked her to write them down, so I could be sure to get it right. I thought I could remember: Which vegetables took longer to cook? Did the potatoes go in first or last? And how about tomatoes? She always added tomato juice from the canning shelves in the basement, but did the tomato juice go in first? It wasn't like it needed to get soft, not like beans and potatoes. Did she also put in tomatoes from the field? I knew corn went into the soup, because Mother said I should shuck it and leave it for her to cut off the cob when she got back.

I pulled the splattered cookbook off the shelf and found recipes for vegetable soup, but none of them looked right, not like the kind of soup we made. One of them didn't have you add beans or corn, and another had you put in peppers, which I knew Mother didn't do, although we had a whole row of them growing in the garden. All of them said you should put in celery, and we grew that in the garden, but it wasn't ready.

Most of the vegetables were in the truck patch, with a few in the garden behind the house. It was a funny thing to call it a truck patch, but I never wondered why we called it that. Maybe it was because we'd pick things and load them into the truck to take to market in Coatesville. We called it "going to market," which was odd too, because market wasn't really a place. Daddy and one of my brothers went door to door with fresh vegetables and eggs. Some people ordered chickens.

I went to market a few times when all my brothers were busy, but I never quite got the hang of it, not like they did. They came home with bubble gum and baseball cards, stories of going out for lunch and buying cold sodas when they got thirsty. The way they talked, they'd go down a whole street all by themselves. The few times I'd gone, I stuck close to Daddy, going only to the houses he told me to go to. He had me knock on the door where the sign on the house said "Tatting." Later, when I told Mother I had gone to Mrs. Tatting's house, she laughed and told me that wasn't her name. The tatting sign meant she made lace. I hoped I hadn't called her Mrs. Tatting to her face, but I didn't know. Daddy asked me to carry the basket of eggs to the rectory, which was next to a church. When I knocked at the door, a man answered. He looked like a priest. They bought a lot of eggs at the rectory.

"Are they Catholics?" I asked Daddy when I went back to the truck.

"Catholics have to eat too."

At our Mennonite church, the preachers didn't have many good things to say about Catholics. They said the Catholics were way off base, the way they worshipped the pope and the Virgin Mary instead of God and Jesus. The man at the rectory was friendly and helped take the eggs from the basket and put them into a big bowl, careful not to crack them.

When I went along to market, I gave Daddy all the money the customers gave me, every cent. I'm sure my brothers turned in most of the money, but they always seemed to have some left in their pockets to buy whatever they wanted. How could I spend money from my pockets when I didn't have any pockets? If I'd had pockets, I'd like to carry a little loose change, some Chiclets, Life Savers, and the tiny tablet I'd gotten as a prize in the Cracker Jack box from the zoo. There was hardly space for a single word on the little page, but sometimes a word was all it took. I was sure I could find a nub of a pencil somewhere. I'd want a pencil in my pocket too. Strange that girls had no pockets.

I'd be on my own out in the field, and no one would know or care if I got hungry or thirsty. As I finished making a bologna sandwich and filling a Mason jar with ice water, I could hear the soup bones begin to rattle in the pot. I loaded the rusted red wagon with containers: plastic bowls, berry baskets, tin buckets. I got the shovel I'd need to dig potatoes and put on my old shoes. You couldn't push down on a shovel with bare feet.

As I went past the barn, I saw my brother Dale cleaning the cow stalls, shoving the manure into the gutter in the stable. I heard the drone of the tractor in the field behind the barn, where Ray was harrowing. Daddy had gone to the feed mill. On our farm, boys' work was a separate thing from girls' work. Boys were mostly in charge of the barn, the cows, anything having to do with tractors and equipment. The house and food-related tasks were girls' work. Only occasionally was there overlap.

My brothers did not know I was making vegetable soup. Dale was older than I was, but he wouldn't have known the first thing about making soup. He would not have known you add tomato juice to the broth, probably never thought about it, all those times he'd eaten vegetable soup. And cabbage, I'm sure he wouldn't have thought about cabbage being in the soup, because it all fell apart when it cooked, and didn't even look like cabbage. If Ray thought about soup, looked at it spoon by spoon, he might have figured out what was in it, because he was interested in studying things, but still, he wouldn't have known how to make it. Maybe boys could drive tractors and clean stables, but, as far as I'd ever seen, there was no way they could make soup.

The containers and shovel clanged as I pulled the rusty metal wagon over the ruts in the back lane past the orchard to the opening in the fence by the truck patch. From the end of the long field, stretching from the back lane to the Amish neighbor's fence line, I could see all the different shades of green. I knew where everything was in the big field. When we'd planted the seeds, the field was soft brown dirt, and the plants had come up in tidy rows. Now the brown had disappeared under all the green. The cantaloupe and watermelon vines had crept across the rows into the tomatoes. Bees darted in and out of the blossoms. The vining lima beans had climbed to the top of the poles, creating shaded teepees. The green in the shade under the lima-bean tents was so dark it was almost black.

I started with potatoes. It was hard digging them. The shovel was taller than I was, and I had trouble pressing it down far enough to get to the big ones. I jumped on it with both feet to make it go deeper. I pulled up the plants, and tiny potatoes clung to the roots. I picked them off and put them in the molasses bucket. They were so small, all I would need to do was wash them and throw them into the soup whole. The dirt was loose, and I could have gotten plenty by pulling up plants. But lots would be missed if I did it without using the shovel. For the good ones, the big ones, Mother said, you had to dig deeper. If you don't get them all as you go along, they'd go to waste. I found a few bigger ones, digging with the shovel and with my hands, but I'm sure I missed some.

When the molasses bucket was full of potatoes, I twisted off a head of cabbage from the next row. I should have brought a knife to cut it off and tried to be careful not to pull up the whole plant. The cabbage heads were still small, so I took a second one and put them both in the wagon.

I filled the wagon slowly—with potatoes and tomatoes, cabbage, lima beans, corn. I left the corn and lima beans for last. Mother always said to keep those for later in the morning because you could pick them in the shade. The corn was taller than I was and kept some of the sun off, and under the lima-bean tents it was shaded and cool.

When I finished picking and digging everything, I pulled the wagon under a tree at the end of the field and sat down to have lunch. I rubbed the dirt off a tomato and bit into it, like an apple, the way I'd seen my brothers do. It made me feel like a farmer. The juice ran down my face, and I wiped it on my sleeve. I ate my sandwich and drank water from the jar. All of the ice had melted, but it was still cool.

I looked over the vegetables in the wagon to make sure I had what I needed from the field before I went to the garden behind the house to pick the rest. I never knew why some things were planted in the garden and some things in the field. Why were the pickles in their own patch by the orchard? And the strawberries next to the pickles? And why were the raspberries and asparagus in the patch in front of the barnyard next to the milk house? Everything had its place, and I knew where to find all of it.

As I pulled the wagon toward the gate at the end of the field, I noticed the buttonweeds growing along the fence. The little green buttonweeds weren't even as big as a pea, and I had, when I was younger, often picked them and served them to my family as a special treat. I would set the table and carefully put a few on the rim of everyone's plate. After I'd taken off the little leaves on the outside, they looked like tiny green buttons. My big brothers laughed when they ate theirs, pretending they were something special. Mother always said how delicious they were and ate every one I'd put on her plate before she ate another thing. I ate all of mine too. I liked buttonweeds. They tasted like raw peas or lima beans. I stopped and picked all I could find along the fence row, and put them in the smallest bowl, the red plastic one. They didn't fill it, but it was almost a cup. No way they would ruin the soup. With all the shapes and sizes and colors and flavors, probably no one would notice, but I would know.

With the wagon loaded with vegetables, it didn't rattle nearly as much as it had when I went out to the field. I pulled it down the back lane and went behind the house to pick green beans, onions, and carrots from the garden. Every container was full.

I carried all of it into the kitchen, where I could smell the soup bones cooking. I took Mother's apron off the hook by the door and tied it on. It went almost to the floor, and I needed to wrap the long strings around and tie them in front. I left the soup bones simmering while I washed and shelled and peeled and chopped. I was careful with the peeler and knife, careful when I fished the soup bones out of the hot broth with the slotted spoon and added the vegetables. I put the but-tonweeds in last. They were small and wouldn't take long to cook. I husked and silked the corn and left it for Mother to cut off the cob, the way she'd asked me.

By the time she came home, everything in the soup pot was simmer-ing together, and it smelled exactly right. I had cleaned up the kitchen, taken all the pods and peels and husks out to the ash pile at the end of the back walk. Although there were no ashes in the summertime, we called it the ash pile all year long.

Mother lifted the lid, looked at the soup, stirred it, and said I had done a good job. She added the corn she'd cut off the cobs, got a pack of the peas we had frozen in the spring, and put those in too. She threw in salt and pepper.

Nancy and Sanford showed me their new shoes. They were nothing special, but they were new. I wished I had new shoes, but my time would come. I knew what the new school shoes would look like: plain brown lace-up shoes. The salesman would measure my feet, press on my toes. I'd probably need the next size because my old shoes were too tight. There would be more market money for shoes, and there would be time to go shopping before school started. When there was soup to be made, shoes could wait.

So many times I'd wished we'd get our soup from those red-and-white cans, like some of my friends did, but that day I didn't think about soup in cans, just the big pot of steaming, simmering vegetable soup I'd made by myself.

When Daddy and my brothers came in from the barn after milk-ing, hungry, as Mother said they would be, they washed their hands at the basin in the corner of the kitchen next to the refrigerator and sat down at the table. After we had silent grace, Mother dipped soup into the bowls, and I carried them to everyone. I could see my chunks of potato were not as neat as Mother's careful cubes when she cut up potatoes for soup, but no one seemed to notice, and no one said anything about the soup tasting different. I knew Mother would not have put buttonweeds in her soup. It's just not what you did. No one mentioned the buttonweeds, and I thought the vegetable soup tasted as good as Mother's. I knew it wasn't the same as hers, and the difference made it taste even better.

It must have been a heady feeling, knowing I could feed my entire family, even if I was only ten years old, that I could do something my mother did, but do it my own way, and no one noticed the difference.

# Yearnings

The farm where I grew up stood on top of a hill overlooking the town of Gap. Who knows what the population might have been. A hundred? A thousand? Maybe more. I was eleven years old, and it was hard enough for me to keep track of how many people lived under the roof of our farmhouse as older brothers and sisters moved away and on to careers and families of their own. Rhoda, Abe, Ike, Jim, and Milt were all gone. My older sister Grace still slept at home, but she was gone most of the time, working, sometimes late into the night, at Dutch Haven, where she was a waitress and baked shoo-fly pies. That summer, if you counted Grace, nine of us still lived at home.

Gap had three streets I remember—Bellevue, Pequea, and Chestnut —but it didn't really matter. They were not our streets. They were the streets in the nearest town, but the town didn't feel like ours. The heart of the town, the business district if it had one, consisted of the bank, post office, and hardware store, with the firehouse down the hill.

The most important street to us was Jesse's back lane, a farm lane running along the edge of a neighbor's fields. It was the most direct route to walk to school, to the bookmobile that came and parked by the town clock every two weeks in summer, and to Lawrence's Store, our main connection to town. We younger children all wanted the chore of walking down Jesse's back lane to Lawrence's to pick up something for Mother—root beer extract, yeast or junket tablets to make ice cream, some small thing easy for a child to carry on the mile-long walk.

Our lives, especially in the summer, were mostly limited to the farm and, of course, church. Some summers we took a one-day trip to the Philadelphia Zoo. After morning milking was finished, we'd pack a lunch and set off for Philadelphia. We would often stop at a church-yard on the way to eat our picnic; sometimes we had it at the zoo. For a treat in the afternoon, we all got to buy Cracker Jacks. The surprises in the box were never as exciting as the anticipation of them—miniature books, plastic whistle rings that scarcely made a sound, miniature mag-nifying glasses. It wasn't so much what it was as the surprise of it. We watched the monkeys play on "Monkey Island," the lions and tigers pac-ing back and forth on the hot dirt outside their cages. In the heat, every-thing smelled a little like the barnyard back on the farm but different. My older brothers stayed home to start the evening milking, and the rest of us were always home by suppertime. It wasn't much, but back then those infrequent outings seemed exciting, a break from summer chores.

It was midafternoon. The hay was raked, and it was too early for my brothers to start the barn work. My mother, brothers, sister, and I sat on the shaded porch shelling the peas we had picked that morning, two half-bushel baskets.

From where I sat on the porch, I could see Suzanne's house on the opposite hill, beyond Jesse's back lane, Lawrence's Store, and the three streets of Gap. Suzanne was in my class at school, and she and her fam-ily lived in an almost-new gray stone ranch house on Strasburg Road. I thought her house was a mansion. I wanted to be her best friend, but I wasn't. How could I be? Best friends played at each other's houses, watched television together, or went to the swimming pool. I did none of those. I looked across at Suzanne's house and wondered what she was doing. She might be inside watching "American Bandstand" with Linda, who lived a few doors down. They might have gotten popsicles from the freezer, or each of them could be sipping Coca-Cola from a green bottle. Maybe she was at Girl Scouts, wearing her pretty green uniform with all those badges she had earned, proving how many things she could do. I wasn't allowed to join Girl Scouts. A couple years earlier I had begged to join Girl Scouts, and Mother said no.

"What's wrong with Girl Scouts?" I said.

"It's not so much that anything's wrong, as what's the use," she said. "Seems like a waste of time and money for all you get out of it."

"They do lots of fun things and get badges for things they learn."

"Just because you don't have a badge for it doesn't mean you don't know how to do things. You know how to do plenty."

I stopped asking about joining Girl Scouts. Of course, I could do things, but I was certain none of the things I knew how to do were badge-worthy. You couldn't get a badge for gathering eggs or picking peas or peeling potatoes.

The porch chairs were in a semicircle, the empty basket for pea pods in the middle. We snapped the crisp pods open, scooped the peas into the bowls we held in our laps, and tossed the empty pods into the basket.

"Let's play a game," Nancy said. "How about 'I'm Going to Grandma's House'?" It was a good game, even for little kids, and made the job go faster. I was good at it, hardly ever missed a word when I tried to remember the whole list.

"All right," Mother said. "You go first."

"I'm going to Grandma's house, and I'm taking an alligator," Nancy said. She threw a pea pod at the basket and missed.

"You can leave it," Mother said, "I'm sure it won't be the only one."

"I'm going to Grandma's house, and I'm taking an alligator and a baseball glove," Sanford said.

"You don't even have a baseball glove," Dale said.

"Nancy doesn't have an alligator either. It doesn't matter."

"Let's just play the game," Mother said, looking up.

It was my older brother Charles's turn. "I'm going to Grandma's house, and I'm taking an alligator, a baseball glove, and calcium."

"Calcium? What's calcium?" I said. "You can't make stuff up."

"I didn't. It's an important chemical element," Charles said. "You'll understand when you take chemistry." He threw his pea pod into the basket.

"I'm going to Grandma's house, and I'm taking an alligator, a baseball glove, calcium, and a dishcloth," Mother said.

She always said things like that when we played the game. Thimble, quilt, hoe, paring knife. If Suzanne's mother played "I'm Going to Grandma's House"—and who could even imagine it—she'd say things like lipstick, hair rollers, pedal pushers, certainly not thimble or dishcloth.

"I'm going to Grandma's house, and I'm taking an alligator, a baseball glove, calcium, a dishcloth, and an encyclopedia," Dale said.

"I bet you can't even spell encyclopedia," Ray said.

"Maybe I can, and maybe I can't. I know it starts with an E."

We made it all the way to Q, where Ray added quartz to the list, but forgot to say ice cube, which I had added. He said he did it on purpose because the ice cube had melted on the way to Grandma's house, but we all knew that was just an excuse. He had lost the game. I was glad, because he thought he was so smart.

The game was over, and my brothers left to start the barn work. They'd clean the stables and bring the cows in from the pasture to feed and milk. Nancy and I helped Mother finish shelling peas. After she'd blanched them, we scooped them into freezer bags. She counted the bags and wrote the number on her list before putting them in the freezer.

The week before I had asked Mother if I could go play at Suzanne's house. I could have walked down Jesse's back lane, across the Lincoln Highway, up Pequea Avenue and across the bridge over the railroad tracks to Strasburg Road. I was old enough to look both ways for cars.

"We have things to do," Mother had said. "We need to freeze these strawberries." I had helped pick them all morning and felt like I had done enough. Why couldn't I have time to go play at Suzanne's or finish reading my Nancy Drew book?

"You know," she said, "I almost feel sorry for those girls. Nothing to do for the whole summer."

I knew we had lots to do. From planting the first seeds in March until we dug the potatoes and cut the cabbage to make sauerkraut in October, the work never ended. And each of us had to do our share. Girls were expected to help can and freeze hundreds of quarts of every fruit and vegetable you can imagine to take us through the winter. The shelves in the basement were full by fall, and when the freezer in the garage filled up, we rented space at Byler's Lockers in town for the overflow.

I knew our family didn't have much money, and we often had to wear clothes older siblings had grown out of, but we were never lacking for food. Mother talked about people who were so poor they didn't get enough to eat, which did not seem possible. We weren't that kind of poor. For us, it was as if food and money had nothing to do with each other.

Sometimes I wondered, but didn't ask, why, if we had so much work to do, my parents always had time for church: Sunday morning and Sunday evening, Prayer Meeting on Wednesday, Sewing School on Saturday, and Summer Bible School every evening for two weeks. If a special prayer meeting was called because someone was sick, my parents always had time for praying, no matter what evening it was or how busy we were or how sick the person was. If the church was open, my parents were there.

After the peas were in the freezer, I went out to gather eggs from the nests in the chicken houses opposite the hayloft. I reached under clucking, pecking leghorns to grab still-warm eggs and place them in the wire basket. I was supposed to count the eggs, but often thought about other things and lost count. I'd make up a number to give Mother, who liked to keep track. If the basket was almost full, I said it was 230, or 215, or 203, always a different number to make it sound like I had counted exactly. When I finished gathering the eggs, looking in all the nests, I went down the stairs and through the barn. Out the front barn doors, left open for summer ventilation, across the cornfield, I could see Suzanne's house.

There was a car in the driveway. It couldn't be her mother's new convertible, the one Suzanne's father got for her at the Oldsmobile dealership where he worked. She always kept the new car in the garage. Maybe it was Joyce's mother's car. She may have come to pick up Joyce, and went inside to chat with Suzanne's mother and have a glass of iced tea. They might be talking about shopping and movies, hairstyles and vacations, things Mother could never have talked about.

I'd seen the new white convertible the day Suzanne's mother picked it up and came by with the top down to get Suzanne from school. It was the first convertible I'd ever seen up close. We never had new cars. My father had bought our somber black Buick from a funeral director in Coatesville who was one of our regular customers for eggs and fresh vegetables. We piled into the Buick to go to church on Sunday. I had to sit forward on the back seat, wedged between long-legged brothers.

I took the basket of eggs into the house and wrote 211 on Mother's list. I carried the basket down to the cellar where Nancy and I cleaned and weighed the eggs before we put them in crates to be sold, layer after layer separated by cardboard dividers.

The next day was haymaking day. The alfalfa had been mowed, crimped, and raked into rows. We'd had a string of hot sunny days, which was perfect weather for haymaking. We all knew the danger of putting away damp hay. We had seen barn fires light up the night sky. If the fire happened during a storm, it was, no doubt, a lightning strike. But, if there was no storm, and we heard the fire siren and saw the eerie glow off in the distance somewhere, Daddy would say, "Probably hot hay." We feared the least moisture left in the hay could lead to hot hay. I had no idea how it worked, but Charles said it was like with the silage, only hotter. I had seen the silage steaming when it came from the silo.

That morning Daddy had pulled the clanging baler back and forth, scooping up the rows of well-dried hay. The bales spewed out and now lay scattered over the dry stubble of the hayfield. At lunch Daddy said, "I need to go to the mill this afternoon. Mary Alice, we need you to drive the tractor to pick up bales. All you need to do is keep it going straight."

I'd helped with haymaking before, and my job had always been to roll the bales into rows. I hated it—the heat and dust and bugs. And the dried hay scratched my arms and the part of my legs not covered by a long skirt. The bales were too heavy for me to lift, but I could roll them. I had never driven the tractor, which was always boys' work. Up on the tractor, I wouldn't get scratched at all.

I went out to the hayfield with my brothers, riding on the edge of the wagon while Ray drove the tractor. When we got to the field, he turned the tractor off, jumped down.

"Get up there," he said, "if you're gonna drive."

I climbed up, and Ray stood on the hitch bar behind me.

"Okay. Push the clutch in far as you can."

I could hardly reach it. I slid down on the smooth metal seat, my skirt bunching up under me. I stretched to get to the clutch and pushed it in. Ray pulled the starter. The tractor chugged to life. He reached past me and pushed the accelerator knob to the second notch.

"Ease up on the clutch and steer. Keep it straight. I'll help you turn when we get to the end."

The tractor only jerked a little as I eased my foot off the clutch and started moving slowly down the row. Ray jumped off the hitch bar and onto the wagon to stack the bales. Dale and Charles, their T-shirts already wet with sweat, tossed the bales onto the wagon. Sanford was far down the field rolling bales into rows. At the end of the first row, Ray helped steer the tractor wide and down the next row.

From the end of the field, up on the rise, I could see across to Strasburg Road, where I thought I saw a bike coming down Suzanne's driveway. Maybe she was going to Sandy's house, where they'd do each other's hair or work on a tap dance routine for the fall talent show at the Gap Fire Hall. I hadn't started to think about what I'd do for the talent show. I'd probably bake a cake again; I might try a chocolate chiffon this time, something harder than the Tiptop Cake I'd made the year before. How could you even compare baking a cake and tap dancing?

I kept the tractor in the second notch and kept it going straight. I knew how fast the tractor could go, had seen my brothers speeding down the lane. All I would need to do was figure out how to change gears and push the accelerator up to the top notch, and bales and brothers would be strewn all over the hayfield. I didn't know how to change gears and wouldn't have considered doing it. My brother trusted me to keep it in the second notch.

"You think you can do the turn at the end?" Ray called from the wagon, now half-filled with bales stacked four high.

"Sure," I said.

I kept the turn wide, lined the tractor and wagon up in the next row. I had to pay attention to what I was doing and couldn't look across to see if anything was happening at Suzanne's house.

I did not then imagine my brothers thinking about anything but hay-making and getting it done right as they loaded the bales. Could Charles, as he tossed bales onto the wagon for Ray to stack, have already been thinking about how he might become a doctor? Might Ray have been dreaming of being a veterinarian like Dr. Breyer? And Dale, was he imagining becoming a businessman? Even Sanford, young as he was, might have had dreams. It never occurred to me, and we seldom talked about it, but, as it turned out, back then all of us must have had imaginings bigger than the boundaries of the farm, and many of those dreams may have gone far beyond Suzanne's hill.

Someone looking on the scene from the outside may have seen only a group of healthy, responsible, contented farm children working together to get the job done, and we were that, but there may have been more going on than I ever thought about.

In the evening after supper we made ice cream, taking turns cranking the freezer and adding salt and ice as it melted down. When the ice cream was almost finished, too stiff for me to turn the handle, my mother added fresh strawberries. We sat on the porch and ate ice cream as the fireflies twinkled beyond the morning glory vines.

From my bedroom window that night, after I had turned off the light, I could see across the valley, beyond the corn field and the wheat field, beyond Jesse's back lane and the streets of town. I thought I could see Suzanne's bedroom window. Her light was still on.

# Wrestling with Peace

I remember that day in sixth grade at Gap Elementary School with painful clarity. Mrs. Groff turned from the board where she had written in her careful cursive the names of the countries involved in the war—seemed pretty much the whole world—and she asked, "How many of your fathers fought in the war?" She might as well have asked, "And how many of your fathers stayed home and milked cows while brave men went off to foreign lands to fight for freedom?" That's how I heard her question. I was embarrassed and wished I could disappear.

It was Veteran's Day, and we were the first wave of "baby boomers" born after the soldiers returned home at the end of World War II. When someone talked about "the war," no question which one it was.

Although hands went up all over the classroom when she asked her question, mine was not the only one that stayed down. We had eight Amish students in my class, and they did not have soldier fathers; and I was not the only one in that sixth-grade class from a Mennonite family.

I copied down the list of countries in case we needed to know them for the test. I could memorize lists. I had already memorized the list of all the books in the Bible, the Old and New Testaments, including the ones you never heard about like Nahum and Habakkuk. A list of countries wouldn't be any trouble.

If someone asked me for a list of things that embarrassed me, I could have given you that list easily, without any memorizing. It was a list that would grow longer in junior high and high school, but in sixth grade, it would have included handmade dresses and hair pulled back into tight French braids—with no hope of bangs. In autumn, I was embarrassed when my hands were stained by black walnuts we picked up under the trees on the fencerow by the thicket, stains no amount of tar soap could wash off. And there were all those brothers and sisters, every two years. Teachers would look up from the list when they saw the name, and I was sure they were thinking, "Another Hostetter." And now I could add to my list of embarrassments a father who had not gone to war.

Maybe no one was looking at me that day in sixth grade, but I was certain the only thing anyone was paying attention to was my hand not being raised. The way I saw it, those of us who did not raise our hands might as well have been painted a cowardly yellow, as some of the Mennonite churches had been by vandals during the war. I wasn't around, but Mother said the buildings were vandalized "because of the church's peace testimony," and the way she said it, it was as if she thought it was a good thing. How could suffering or being embarrassed for your beliefs be something you'd want?

It wasn't the first time our church's troublesome "peace testimony" caused me problems. It had come up with the safety patrol too, an organization that, as far as I could tell, had no connection whatsoever to war. We were allowed to participate in the safety patrol, which had the weighty responsibility of keeping the other students orderly as they went back into the school after recess or a fire drill. I proudly wore my white safety patrol sash, the diagonal band holding the blue pin when I was chosen to be captain.

The problem was that students in the safety patrol were invited to participate in parades in our small town, and members of my family were not allowed to have anything to do with parades. Participating in parades, or attending them, was nonnegotiable.

"Parades are about glorifying the military," Mother said. "And you don't need to be marching down the street with those half-dressed majorette girls either."

Even beyond sixth grade, I made an uneasy peace with the pacifism that was part of my heritage, mostly hoping no one would notice my family's lack of patriotic fervor. No flags flew at our farm on the hill overlooking Gap on patriotic holidays. No flags adorned the graves of generations of ancestors buried in Hershey's Mennonite Church cemetery. None of my eight brothers served in the military; neither had any of my uncles. Some of them participated in alternative service as conscientious objectors, working in hospitals, or building trails in national parks.

Often, on our way to visit Aunt Mabel and Uncle Clarence, who lived a few farms away, we drove by the VFW building across from Lengacher's Cheese House on Route 30. There were almost always cars and trucks in the parking lot, but we seldom saw anyone going in or out. I always wondered what went on at the VFW and once asked Daddy. "They probably do a lot of drinking," he said.

I wouldn't have known it then, but the peace testimony would interfere again when, in my senior year of high school, I won the DAR Good Citizens Award. The day I heard I was chosen, I hurried home to tell Mother.

"Guess what, I got picked to be the DAR Good Citizen. And you'll be invited to the award lunch at the Iris Club."

"I don't think anyone in this family is a Daughter of the American Revolution," she said.

I hadn't considered what DAR stood for, choosing to focus on the "good citizen" part, and especially the award part, which meant they would give me money.

"It's just the name of their group," I said. "It doesn't mean anything."

Mother, standing over the sink in her long, faded-cotton dress and apron, stopped peeling potatoes and looked at me.

"Of course it means something."

I spread the red-checked tablecloth on the kitchen table and smoothed it. "It's a bunch of women who want to give an award to a student they think made a difference, and my teachers picked me. That's all. I thought you'd be happy."

"I'm not saying they don't do some good things. But they're in the group because they want to glorify war."

She put the potatoes on the stove, turned on the burner.

"I won't keep you from going to get your award," she said, "but I don't think I'll be having lunch at the Iris Club with the DAR. They're not my people."

I knew I would be going to the luncheon alone. I couldn't change Mother's mind, although I considered saying something like "When all the mothers get introduced, I'll tell them I'm an orphan." I was allowed to go to the ceremony, and I knew it was the most I could hope for. I don't remember much about the event, what we had for lunch, or who spoke or gave us our awards. But I'm fairly certain I was the only Mennonite among the students being honored that day.

When I was young, it seemed to me most of the people considered heroes had at some time worn a military uniform. Because of its strict pacifist beliefs, the Mennonite Church understandably did not have any heroes in uniforms. What we had instead was an abundance of martyrs, a whole book of them.

No book in our living room bookcase other than the Bible was treated with more reverence than a book called *The Martyrs' Mirror*, with page after page of stories and illustrations about all the people in the history of our church who were tortured and killed for what they believed. The book was almost as big as the family Bible, and the illustrations showed burnings, beheadings, hangings, and other brutal and gruesome deaths. It was not really a children's book, but we looked at it often. I found the book, especially the vivid illustrations, awful and fascinating, showing all the ways people could be tortured and killed. But they were martyrs, not heroes.

One especially compelling story in the book was about a martyr named Dirk Willems. He was part of a group called the Anabaptists, who in sixteenth-century Europe rebelled against the beliefs of both Catholicism and the Protestant Reformation. The Mennonites evolved from that group. Everyone hated the Anabaptists, it seemed, and they were persecuted without mercy. Dirk Willems was in prison for his beliefs, which no amount of torture would make him renounce. He escaped and fled across a frozen lake, a guard pursuing him. Dirk made it across, but the guard fell through the ice and called for help. Dirk heard his cries and went back to rescue him from the icy water. He saved his pursuer's life, but Dirk was recaptured and burned at the stake. The illustration in *The Martyrs' Mirror* shows him pulling the man from the lake. The lesson we were to learn? I wasn't sure. In spite of doing the right thing, you might still be tortured and killed. No wonder I couldn't think of martyrs as heroes.

On the shelf above *The Martyrs' Mirror* in the bookcase was *Paul the Peddler*, a book by Horatio Alger. We had read that book so often the worn cover was falling off. Paul the Peddler's fate was happier than Dirk's. Paul was a poor boy, sometimes living on the street, and the other boys were often cruel to him. He had worked hard to make his way, and a wealthy man noticed him one day and set him up in his own business. Everything turned out just fine for Paul the Peddler. He thrived and showed the boys who had tormented him that he was not defeated.

The way I understood it then, within the Christian Church, and especially in the Anabaptist branch of that group, dying for what you believed, no matter how gruesome the death, added credibility to your beliefs. I probably shouldn't have compared Paul the Peddler to martyrs like Stephen, who was stoned to death for his beliefs, or John the Baptist, who was beheaded for speaking out against King Herod, or even Dirk Willems, who risked death with his act of compassion. But that's what came to mind, and I could not understand why they were not all rewarded for doing the right thing.

When I was growing up, issues around peace seemed so black and white. It was simple. All you needed to do to support peace was avoid parades and any activity requiring a uniform, including the Girl Scouts. It went without saying that you could have nothing to do with war. As for martyrs, they all seemed part of a distant history having nothing to do with me. The heroes in uniform were far more exciting to me, even though I knew I could not claim them.

Back then I could not have imagined there would come a time when I would choose to study writings of nonviolent resistance, teach those writings, or be drawn to faith groups because of their pacifist teachings.

# PART TWO

# Simple Pleasure

It was a Sunday afternoon in June, and I was twelve. We had spent the morning at church, had a big Sunday dinner, and the afternoon was a time without chores, without church, without expectations. The wheat in the field on the hill was already glowing golden as I gathered up a blanket and book and walked up the path to the meadow. No one was watching.

At the top of the hill I turned left, toward the woods, and went through the gate and around to the far side of the field. When I was sure I was out of sight of the house, I went into the wheat, almost waist high. I could imagine my father's voice, "Don't trample the wheat," but I didn't care. I knew my path would be hidden.

When I got deep into the field, I spread my blanket and took out my book. I unbuttoned my blouse and took it off, pulled my skirt up above my knees. Mother's admonitions about modesty echoed faintly in my mind as I lay down on the blanket, the sun warming my legs and arms and shoulders as I opened my book and started reading. I had gotten the book from the bookmobile when it came to town on Thursday. Sanford and I walked down Jesse's back lane and up the Gap Hill to pick out our books.

"Try to find a book that's edifying," Mother had said.

I checked out *Green Mansions*, and Sanford chose *The Story of Babe Ruth*.

Lying in the sun, in the ripening wheat, on that golden Sunday afternoon, with skin exposed for no one but God to see, I read. I felt almost
invisible. If no one could see me, surely it could not count as immodest.
I could hear the grasshoppers, the click bugs, the rustling of the wheat.
With sun on shoulders that had never before felt the sun, I lost myself
in the exotic world of a South American rain forest and the unlikely tale
of a young adventurer falling in love with an otherworldly bird girl.

Later in the afternoon I put my blouse back on, folded my blanket,
and went down the lane to the house, going in the back door and up to
my room. I had disappeared for hours, and no one had even noticed.

When Ira, who hired out with his combine, came to harvest the
wheat in a couple weeks, to shake out the grain and leave the straw
to be baled, I doubt he'd notice from his perch up on top of his big
machine that a path had been trampled into the center of the field and
the wheat flattened where I'd spread my blanket. Only I would know,
remembering how good the sun felt on my bare shoulders and legs,
savoring my delicious secret.

# Billy Graham's Necktie

In our family we did not often slam doors, raise voices, or shed tears. If Mother burned the bacon or dropped a plate, and it shattered on the kitchen floor, she might on rare occasions quietly mutter, "Oh, fiddlefart," which was as strong as her language got. So, when I walked by my parents' closed bedroom door one fall evening and heard what sounded like Mother crying, I was surprised and stopped to listen. They were praying, as they did every evening before they went to sleep, but it was usually silent, Daddy kneeling on one side of the bed, Mother on the other. I heard Mother, through her quiet sobs, praying aloud, "and help her to heed the call of the Spirit and accept Christ as her personal Savior."

I knew she was talking about me. I was fourteen that fall revival season. Most of the kids my age in our church, as well as my older siblings, had already accepted Christ as their personal Savior and joined the Mennonite Church. It was my turn. My time. My parents had gone to the revivals each evening. There were only a few more services before the evangelist, who had traveled from upstate Pennsylvania to our community in the southeastern part of the state, would move on to the next church.

I sneaked down the hallway and back to my bedroom. I knelt quickly by the bed to say my prayers. When I got to "If I should die before I wake, I pray thee, Lord, my soul to take," I wondered if praying that prayer would even make a difference for me. I climbed into bed beside

Nancy. I remembered the evangelist's sermon from the first night of the revivals, the only one I'd gone to. He read from the Bible: "Two shall be sleeping in a bed; one will be taken; the other will be left." He had looked out across the congregation and asked, "If the Lord returned today, are you ready, or will you be left behind?" I could hear Nancy breathing in the darkness beside me. She was only ten, probably too young to be left to burn in hell. Although she often annoyed me, begging me to play dolls with her or rolling over onto my side of the bed while she slept, I didn't want to be separated from her for all eternity.

At the first night's revival, the evangelist had said, "The latter days are upon us, and it is time for us to look out for our souls, lest we be tossed into the fiery pit, where the flames will not be quenched." He said he knew some of us had reached "the age of accountability" and should heed the call of the Holy Spirit. I wondered if he could be talking about me.

The whole "age of accountability" issue didn't make sense—the idea that one day you were innocent, and the next day, with nothing changing about how you lived your life, you needed to be "born again" or you would be tossed into the everlasting fires of hell. I guessed there had to be the one before-and-after-moment that made the difference between innocent and damned. It didn't seem fair. For all the times I had heard preachers talking about needing to be born again, I didn't know what it really meant.

Lying in the darkness, filled with fear, I could almost feel the heat of hell's fire, and I had trouble getting to sleep. If hell had been in Mother's precipice story, I imagined the sheer edge would have dropped off into a fiery chasm. What if the Second Coming happened overnight? I thought I remembered the Bible saying there would be trumpets. If I was not one of those taken, would I hear the trumpets? Maybe only the righteous or the innocent would hear them, and the rest would wake up and find everyone else gone. If I was the only one left behind in my family, I knew I couldn't take care of the cows and the chickens all by myself. No one could. I tried to calm down by thinking of regular things—homework assignments, my science project, notes I needed to write to friends. I counted backward from one hundred, twice, and finally fell asleep.

When I awoke the next morning to bright sunshine, Mother's sobs and all those dark thoughts felt like I had dreamed them. I went downstairs and found Mother working in the kitchen, as usual. Her hair was pulled back in a bun under her prayer covering; she wore a simple printed dress and pale-blue apron. When I came into the kitchen, she looked up and smiled. Nothing in the way she looked or acted gave the slightest hint she thought my soul was doomed.

"After you've had breakfast, could you mix up a cake while I finish these pies?" she said.

"Sure." I was relieved to have things feel normal.

"I think we're almost ready for tomorrow," she said. "We can set the dining room table later."

"What's tomorrow?"

"Didn't I tell you? The evangelist and his wife are coming."

"Oh."

I finished mixing the cake, she crimped the crusts for the lemon sponge pies, and we put all of it in the oven. Mother set the timer.

Then, in a tone I'm not sure I'd ever heard from her before, she said, "There's something I need to talk to you about." She took off her apron and draped it over the back of the kitchen stool. She never took her apron off in the middle of the day, not unless she'd run out of flour or brown sugar and needed to go to the store.

I followed her into the living room. She picked up her Bible from the end table and sat down on the sofa. I sat in the chair across from her, wishing the phone would ring or someone would come to the door—anything to interrupt. The phone didn't ring. No one came to the door. My brothers were in the barn helping Daddy clean the stable, and Nancy was still in bed. There was no one to interrupt. With so many brothers and sisters, I had often wished for times I could have Mother all to myself, but not that day. I looked down at her everyday black-leather shoes.

One of them was untied to relieve the pressure on her bunion. I noticed the worn place on the carpet in front of the sofa. The clock on the mantel ticked. It sounded louder than usual.

"When you're growing up," she said, "at your age or younger, you begin to feel the need to accept Christ as your personal Savior. From the beginning of the revivals this year, I have felt the Spirit moving in you."

I stared at her hands, at the pie dough caked around her nails as they rested on her well-used, familiar Bible. Her words sounded strange, talking like a preacher, and I couldn't believe they were coming from her. How could someone so practical be sitting in the living room on a Saturday morning talking about Spirits? She should be baking or canning, cleaning or harvesting, ironing or mending, not talking about Spirits.

She cleared her throat. "Do you have any questions?"

What could I ask? She sounded like the evangelist. How could she be sure it was my time when I wasn't? At first I couldn't think of anything, but I remembered something I had often wondered about, and I blurted out, "What about Billy Graham?" It's not like I'd been thinking about Billy Graham at that moment, but it's what came to mind.

"What about Billy Graham?" She looked confused.

"The thing I was wondering is how Billy Graham can get into heaven wearing a necktie if it's wrong for the men in our church to wear them?"

I had gone on the church bus trip to the Billy Graham Crusade at Connie Mack Stadium in Philadelphia. He'd stood in front of all those thousands of people, talking about being born again, saying pretty much the same thing the evangelist said at our church, and Billy Graham was wearing a necktie. The way Billy Graham talked that night at the crusade, it was almost as if he was personally in charge of who got into heaven. But why was it that the Mennonite preachers and my father and all the adult men in our church were forbidden to wear ties and required to wear specially made suits with no collars, suits buttoned up tight over their white shirts. Why were there different rules for getting into heaven? Billy Graham didn't need to go to the Plain Clothing Department in Hager's Store in Lancaster to buy a special suit like my father did. There seemed to be no doubt of Billy Graham getting into heaven.

Mother stood up and walked across the living room, pulling down the green shade to block the sun from shining on the sofa. She sat down in the rocking chair.

"First of all," she said, "it is not up to us to judge who will get into heaven. On Judgment Day, God will look on the soul, not on what we're wearing."

"I agree with God on that," I said, remembering arguments I'd had with Mother about what I was allowed to wear. I always felt conspicuous in my long homemade skirts or shapeless jumpers. I couldn't understand why looking different was important to the people who made the church rules.

Mother continued, "God is not someone to agree or disagree with. He is to be worshipped, and his will trusted."

"Another thing," I said. "What about people who don't know about Jesus or the Holy Spirit? What will happen to them on Judgment Day?"

"As I understand it, and I'm no expert, they will be treated like the innocent children. God will welcome them into his kingdom. But the most important thing to remember is that if we know the Word, it is our responsibility to spread it to the far reaches of the earth."

I remembered the slides the missionaries had shown when they came home on furlough, pictures of African women in prayer coverings and long plain dresses, rejoicing with the missionaries that their souls had been saved. Somehow the photos of the women still wearing their bright dresses and head scarves felt just as joyous to me, maybe more so.

Mother leaned back and began rocking. The chair creaked in a way that on another day I might have found soothing. What she said didn't clear up much of anything for me. What if those poor, uneducated souls were doing fine in their ignorance?

"What I hope is clear to you," Mother said, "is your first responsibility is for your own soul, not Billy Graham's, and not those people who have never heard the Word. Do you understand?"

"Yes, I think so," I said, but I really didn't understand.

"Now let's have a moment of silent prayer."

We bowed our heads. Her prayer, I'm sure, was for my eternal soul. Mine was for the moment to pass quickly and for the oven timer to buzz.

Mother stood and smoothed her dress. "I'm glad we had this talk," she said, walking toward the kitchen. Then, with scarcely a pause, "Do you think we need pudding for tomorrow, or do you think the pie and cake will be enough?"

"I don't think it matters," I said.

We went on with the day. It was now out in the open that my soul was at risk. I had other questions I might have asked. Hanging over our bed was a framed quote: "God is Love." I had gotten it for memorizing all the books of the Bible. The quote hanging there had always made me feel better. It reminded me of the Bible verses about God taking care of the lilies of the field and the birds of the air, and I was always sure he would take care of me too. I didn't know how it happened that such a happy, kind God one day got so angry that he could throw a fourteen-year-old into everlasting hellfire for no good reason, just because she reached a certain age. How could you turn a thought like that into a question, let alone ask it? Wouldn't a loving God at least give me time to get answers to my questions?

Throughout my childhood, I had confidently walked on the path of righteousness I was certain I had been born on. We sang a song in Sunday school: "One door and only one, and yet its sides are two. I'm on the inside. On which side are you?" I had felt secure about being on the right side. Now, suddenly, without taking a turn or going through the door, it seemed I was on the wrong side if I didn't choose to be born again. How could that happen?

The whole family went to church on Sunday morning. No choice. Our regular minister preached, and he talked about heaven and its pearly gates, what a beautiful place it would be. He didn't mention the fires of hell. The evangelist and his wife sat in the congregation, and after the service they followed us home for noonday dinner. When we arrived, the men went into the living room, and my brothers grabbed the basketball from the garage, taking shots at the basket mounted on the side of the barn. They didn't change out of their Sunday clothes. The evangelist's wife joined Mother and me in the kitchen while we finished preparing the food. They chatted about quilting and gardening and canning and children. I mashed the potatoes, and Nancy watched, pouring in warm milk when I asked her to.

We usually ate at the kitchen table and usually had silent grace. With Sunday guests, we ate in the dining room using the good dishes, and the evangelist said grace.

"We thank you, Lord, for this food, and the loving hands that prepared it for us." Right in the middle of the prayer, where he should have said something about "blessing the food to our use and us to thy service," he went in a whole new direction. "And Lord," he said, in a voice too big for the dining room, "let your Spirit work among us, and, if there are those who would not heed your call, let them not close their ears and hearts to you. In Jesus's name, Amen." After a pause, my father said, "Well, let's dig in."

Earlier, in the kitchen, when I smelled the roast beef and gravy, I couldn't wait to eat. Now I didn't care about the food, not even the cake I made for dessert. I wanted to go to my room and close the door against preachers, the Holy Spirit, and all the pressure to make me feel I was so bad that I needed to be saved. Could that very thought mean I was closing my ears and heart? I stayed at the table.

The evangelist managed to eat two heaping plates of food, all the while telling us about the workings of the Spirit all over the state— the homeless alcoholic, a man in the penitentiary for murder, a woman healed after being paralyzed in an accident. All of those lives had been turned around, but their situations sounded different from mine. My life would be pretty much the same if I was born again. I'd still try to keep up with my schoolwork and get good grades, do my share of the chores and obey my parents. It wasn't like I needed a miracle.

I helped Mother clear off the plates and serve dessert, and finally dinner was finished. When the last of the Sunday dishes were washed and dried and put away, I went to my room to do homework.

I stayed there for the rest of the afternoon, long after I saw the evangelist and his wife drive slowly away down the long lane from our farm.

When I went downstairs for supper, Mother asked if I'd be going along
to the revival that evening.

"I thought I would." I did not want to be seen as one who would
close my ears and my heart to the Word.

We drove through a patchwork of farms and fields, turning onto the
narrow road by the Amish peach orchard. We went up the last hill and
parked in the gravel parking lot by the plain, gray-shingled church.

The church was full for the last evening of the revivals. After all the
benches were filled, the ushers added folding chairs in the aisles. I sat
near the back with some girls my age. If any of them felt the Spirit
moving me, they didn't let on. They had all been born again in past
revivals and joined the church. They sat there with their long hair pulled
back into buns and covered with the prayer coverings girls and women
were required to wear after they joined the church. I thought a prayer
covering would be a nuisance, and I knew I would be embarrassed to
wear one, especially at school. It didn't seem the girls I was sitting with
minded wearing them, but I couldn't really tell. The girls were giggling
about the boys sitting across from us on the men's side, oblivious to my
conflict.

With a larger congregation, the opening hymns, "Onward, Christian
Soldiers" and "Work for the Night Is Coming," were a powerful beginning to the service. I sang with more enthusiasm than usual, caught up
with the increased volume of all the voices. After our regular minister
read the scripture, the evangelist stood up. He grabbed the podium with
hands that looked strong enough to throw boulders. He took a deep
breath, then boomed, "Get thee behind us, Satan; get thee behind us,
Satan." If I had been Satan, I would have left. The girls beside me stopped
whispering.

The sermon, like the one from the service I'd gone to on the first
night of the revivals, drew mostly on verses from the book of Revelation
and all the signs that we were, in fact, living in "the latter days." The
evangelist had no doubt the Antichrist was at work among us. With
the whole world to choose from, I was surprised he would single out
our little church, but, if Satan could be anywhere, surely the Antichrist
could be too. From the invention of the airplane to the atomic bomb,

from Khrushchev to a Catholic being elected president—all were evidence the Second Coming was close at hand. I didn't understand how the evangelist figured it out from verses about horses and beasts and clouds and all sorts of things that didn't seem to be about Russia or airplanes or bombs. But he was sure of himself. The evangelist warned that Satan tempted us with thoughts and doubts and questions. I wondered if the questions I thought were mine might really be put in my mind by Satan. But why would you have thoughts from Satan if it was God who created everything about us, including our minds? Wouldn't God have fixed that? I wondered if Satan might have planted that thought in my mind.

The sermon was long. According to the clock on the wall behind the pulpit, it took thirty-eight minutes. At times I thought the evangelist stared straight at me, and I moved behind the woman in front of me to block his view. After he ended the sermon, he said a prayer and announced the page number for the invitation hymn.

The evangelist, his face red from the exertion of the sermon and the heat with all those people crowded into the small church, looked out over the congregation as we found our places in the hymnals. His plain suit was buttoned all the way up to his thick neck, and you could hardly see the collar of his white shirt. Even if he had been wearing a necktie, you couldn't have seen it.

We stayed seated as we sang, "Softly and Tenderly Jesus Is Calling." It was the same song we sang the evening I went to the Tent Revival in our neighbor's field in the summertime, but it felt different out in the field, under the tent, with the smell of the sawdust, the evening breezes blowing through, and all those people singing so loudly. That evening at the tent meeting I hadn't felt trapped at all, not like I did in the crowded church. In the tent, I could have slipped away under the tent flaps and into the night, and no one would have noticed. Inside the church, with chairs in the aisles and all those people packed in, there was no chance I could slip away.

The evangelist said if anyone wanted to be saved, they could show it by either standing briefly or walking to the front of the church, where he stood singing, his arms outstretched, ready to welcome them to the Kingdom of God.

Robert, a man Mother called "a poor soul," went forward during the first verse of the hymn. I remembered him going forward the year before. He came to church for a few months after the revival and then returned to a life that seemed free of worry about his eternal soul. I wondered what would happen to Robert if the Day of Judgment came during one of his periods of backsliding. Robert knelt in front of the evangelist, who put his hand on his head and moved his lips in prayer. He returned to his seat looking triumphant as we all continued to sing. I should have asked Mother if you needed to be born again more than one time, and why Robert went forward year after year.

I imagined how it would be to stand up quickly, where I was, until the evangelist noticed me. It wouldn't take long. I wouldn't go forward, not like Robert. I didn't want the attention. People would greet me afterward, and it would be embarrassing for a little while. Would it be best to do it and get it over with?

We sang the last verse of the hymn, but I did not stand up to show I wanted to be born again, and I was relieved it was over until next year's revival. Then the evangelist said, "Brothers and sisters, I feel the Spirit moving among us here tonight. Let's stand to sing the last two verses again, and let us sing them prayerfully. If anyone wants to come to the Lord, they may indicate that by remaining standing for a moment at the end of the song as the rest of the congregation is seated." I stood with everyone as we sang, "Time is now fleeting, the moments are passing, passing from you and from me." The evangelist's voice was louder than anyone's.

I remembered what Mother had said in the living room: my only responsibility was to take care of my own soul. How could I remain standing to acknowledge I was a sinner if I didn't feel like one? An all-knowing God would certainly see I wasn't being honest. We sang the last line of the hymn, "calling, oh sinner, come home." I sat down quickly. I felt like everyone was staring at me, sure that I would be the one to remain standing. I had thought this might be the revival that felt like the right time, but I didn't feel any more certain about it than I had before. If I had gone forward or stood up, it would have been to make everyone else feel better. I wondered about all those people sitting around me. Did they think they were sinners before they were born again? My friends who had already joined the church and my older brothers and sisters? When they were baptized, they said they had repented, but what had they repented of? It wasn't something I would ask any of them. We didn't talk about things like that. It felt as if all of them had just done what was expected. I didn't know why I couldn't do that.

The evangelist thanked the congregation for welcoming him and his wife so warmly. He gave the benediction, and the revivals were over for another year. No matter what happened at the next revival or the one after that, this one was over. He stood at the back door and shook hands with everyone as they left the church. When it was my turn, he shook my hand firmly.

"God bless you," he said.

"And you too," I said.

After the heat of the crowded church, the crisp fall air outside was a relief. I stood on the fringes of the group as others carried on quiet conversations. For all I knew, the fires of hell could have been lapping toward my feet at that very moment, but I felt like I had escaped with my life. How could I know for sure? I might be taking a serious chance; I could be running out of time.

No one in my family said anything as we got into our black Buick, my parents and Nancy in the front, my brothers and I in the back. We drove away. The church, still brightly lit on top of the bald hill, stood like a beacon that grew smaller and more distant as we wound our way through the dark countryside. I gazed out the window across the fields at the stars glimmering in the night sky.

# Cleansed at Crystal Flow

I did not go to Crystal Flow Camp the summer I was fifteen with the intention of being born again. I only wanted to go to camp, and a new church camp, less than an hour from where we lived, had opened a couple of years earlier. My parents, no doubt encouraged that I wanted to spend time with Mennonites, surprised me by saying I could go. No one in the family had gone to camp before.

I had always envied my friends who went to Girl Scout camp but knew that wasn't an option for me. Of course, my camp would be a church camp, but it was better than no camp at all.

I paid for some of it from my own money, money I'd saved from trapping mice at a penny a mouse, picking potato bugs off the plants at a nickel-a-jar, and selling radishes from the partial row each of us was assigned in the garden to grow whatever we wanted to sell on our market route. I chose radishes, tied them in little bunches to sell for a nickel. By the time I went to camp, I had savings.

And I had saved allowance money too. I was up to getting a dollar a week, if I did everything I was supposed to. We got nickel or dime deductions for fighting, talking back, slacking on chores. My allowance was occasionally less than a dollar.

I had packed a bathing suit borrowed from a cousin, with a skirt halfway to my knees. I didn't mind. The list of what to bring to camp included "modest bathing suit," and Mother said she'd make one for me, sew it from a fabric remnant. I was sure a borrowed store-bought one was better than homemade.

My parents dropped me off at camp on a Sunday afternoon, and Crystal Flow seemed like a magical place, dark cabins with crowded bunk beds, a dusty baseball field, craft room, cafeteria, a murky lake with a rickety row boat and stacks of inner tubes, and a circle of logs around the fire pit. The list of activities was so long I didn't know how we'd fit them all into a week: Bible study, volleyball, softball, crafts, swimming, badminton, everything you could think of. They sounded like the things my friends talked about doing at Girl Scout camp, although the Girl Scouts probably didn't have devotions in the evening and weren't expected to memorize a Bible verse every day. I already knew most of the verses we needed to memorize, and I think most of the other kids did too. The only chores were making your bed and taking a turn with cleanup after meals. It was like a vacation. There were no eggs to gather, nothing to pick or can or freeze. I couldn't remember ever having a whole week to play.

I was assigned to Pine Cabin. I didn't know any of the other girls in my cabin. Most of them already wore prayer coverings. Only a few of us, it seemed, had not yet joined the church. Since slacks and shorts were not allowed for girls, I didn't feel self-conscious in my shapeless blouses and skirts that covered my knees. All the girls wore similar clothes.

You couldn't tell whether the boys had or hadn't joined the church. They wore regular clothes, had regular haircuts, and looked like everyone else, even after they joined the church. At camp they mostly wore jeans and T-shirts.

Jesus was a big part of the camp, with mottos on the walls everywhere saying things like "Ye are the light of the world," "I can do all things through Christ who strengthens me," and "Jesus Saves." At evening devotions the counselors talked about how we serve Jesus in all we do and say and think. The Jesus everyone talked about seemed like a nice guy, the sort of person who'd catch for both softball teams if you were short on players. It was like Jesus had come to camp on his own, like the rest of us, and left his angry father at home. I'd always seen them as a team: God and Jesus. It was the first time Jesus felt like a separate person, not scary at all. And none of the counselors mentioned hellfire or eternal punishment, not once during the whole week.

Each evening after dinner we had a Bible Bee, with the six cabins competing against each other to answer Bible questions the counselors read from cards. The cards must have been part of a game many campers were already familiar with, especially the girls from Maple Cabin. It was as if they had practiced from the exact cards, which didn't seem fair. I had never heard of the Bible Lotto game and had never seen the cards. Some of the questions were easy, things like "How did the wise men find their way to Bethlehem?" or "What is John 3:16?" Of course, I would have known those. Anybody would. "How many days was Jonah in the whale's belly?" Who doesn't know that?

During one of the evening Bible Bees, when our cabin was not doing well, it was my turn. I stood up. "Where was Paul when he wrote the Epistle to Philemon?" one of the counselors read. What kind of question was that, compared to the wise men's star? It was like a spelling bee where one person was asked to spell "run" and the very next one was asked to spell "miscellaneous." Of course, I knew there was a book in the Bible called Philemon. I had memorized all the books of the Bible. I would have guessed Paul wrote it, since he pretty much wrote a lot of the books in the New Testament, but who knows where he was. He traveled all over the place.

I stood there, paused, as if I was trying to decide between a few of the towns Paul had gone to. Then I said, "Thessalonica," because I liked the sound of it. It felt better to say something, better than "I have no idea," which was the truth.

"No," said the counselor, reading from the back of the card. "Paul was in prison."

At the end of the evening's session, Maple Cabin stayed in first place, and my Pine Cabin slipped to fifth. Only Oak Cabin had fewer points than Pine. Oak was one of the boys' cabins down the hill. They said they didn't care, because they were winning at volleyball.

It was midweek and Glenn's turn to lead the campfire devotions. Everyone liked Glenn, and he was my favorite counselor too, cute and friendly, with blue eyes and an adorable dimple. He wore sandals like I had never seen. I was sure he had gotten them in Africa or some exotic place where he had done his Mennonite Voluntary Service.

"Let's sing 'What a Friend We Have in Jesus,'" Glenn said. His sweet voice rang out as he started the song. "What a friend we have in Jesus, all our sins and griefs to bear." He didn't seem to mind singing by himself before we all joined in. Everyone knew the song, and it felt like Jesus was right there in the fire circle with us. We sang "This Little Light of Mine," not in a round exactly, more like an echo. It sounded beautiful there at the edge of the darkening woods. I don't know how Glenn figured it out. Maybe it was something they did in foreign countries.

After the songs, Glenn led a devotion about serving Jesus. At the end he said, "Let's go around the circle and share what Jesus means to us and how we might better serve him."

The girl sitting on the log nearest to him said, "I want to renew my commitment to serve Jesus. When school starts, I'm not going to laugh if someone says something mean about someone else. I'll remind them Jesus wants us to be kind to one another."

Most of the campers took their cue from her, with lots of variations on commitment, kindness, and witnessing.

As we worked around the circle, and it got closer to being my turn, I knew I had to come up with something to say. It wouldn't be anything about witnessing, I was certain of that. What would witnessing look like? Going up to someone in the hall at school and asking them if they were born again? No, thank you. Being kind was a good idea but sounded a little stupid, since at least half the kids had already said something about kindness. Whatever I said, I didn't want it to sound like I had copied from the other kids.

A shy, nervous boy on the end of the log where I was sitting—I could never remember his name, something like James or John, a disciple name—when it was his turn, said, "I would like to accept Christ as my personal Savior." The counselors, and probably some campers too, said, "Praise Jesus."

It was almost my turn. I could feel the heat from the bonfire on my face, and on my back I could feel the damp night chill. The campers sitting on the log between the shy boy and me promised they were going to serve Jesus better with everything they said and did. Even their thoughts. I was next.

The fire crackled and threw a shower of sparks into the night sky as I said, "I'd like to accept Christ as my personal Savior," and there was again a resounding "Praise Jesus." I thought I could hear Glenn's voice over all of them.

I was so relieved I scarcely heard what the rest of the campers in the circle said. It was like the words had come out of my mouth all by themselves. I hadn't even thought about it. I had finally done it. In the dark with the shaky light from the fire, the other kids may not have known who was talking. I hoped it still counted. No longer would I need to worry about hellfire.

In his prayer at the end of the fireside devotion, before we sang "Blest Be the Tie That Binds," Glenn said, "And we give thanks for the precious souls who gave their hearts to Jesus this evening." I was sure he was thinking of me.

After the bonfire, I walked back to Pine Cabin with Anna and Charlene.

"Glenn is so cute," Anna said. "I saw him swimming down at the lake today after the boys finished. Even his back looks good."

"Yeah," said Charlene. "I almost feel sorry for Harold. He's not bad-looking, but compared to Glenn . . ."

Harold was another one of the guy counselors, a lot quieter than Glenn and a good softball player. No one paid much attention to the girl counselors. They weren't as much fun. Louise, the counselor in our cabin, wasn't any fun at all. Her dresses were almost as plain as Mother's, but not quite as long. It was like she was nervous things might get out of control in Pine Cabin. If someone as much as whispered after lights out, she'd say "Quiet," like she was a schoolteacher or librarian.

We walked back to the cabin, the three of us, discussing the relative good looks of all the guy counselors. No one mentioned my born-again moment. They may not have known it was me, or maybe it was already old news, paling in comparison to Glenn's charm.

We got ready for bed, and Louise turned out the lights. We were all expected to be praying quietly until Louise's "Amen" signaled the end of prayer time. Included in my silent prayer was thanks that the Second Coming had not happened before I was born again.

I was not the kind of person to get things started after lights out, but I was happy to go along with it. Janet would get it going, and it didn't take much. She was in the bunk below mine. She'd say some silly thing to get everyone giggling. The cabin had two windows, and Janet had the best view out one of them. "There's a bear out there," she'd whisper, or "Why is Pastor Hershey looking in the window?" Or she'd say she saw one of the boys no one liked from Oak Cabin down the hill. Everyone said the boys were locked in at night to keep them out of trouble, so I doubted she'd really seen anyone.

"You girls better get quiet, or else," Louise would say, and after a while we'd settle down. I doubt she had a "what else" plan, but she didn't really need one. You can only giggle for a short time when you're tired.

In the quiet I could hear the crinkle of the plastic covers on the mattresses as the other girls moved in their beds. The woods around the cabin were noisy at night . . . but not the same kind of noisy I was used to back on the farm. I wasn't sure what all the woods noises were, but I wasn't scared. At home I knew the outside sounds—the crickets and the wind rustling the corn leaves in the field below my bedroom window. If it was windy, and the pears were ripe, I could hear them dropping to the ground from the trees in the yard. Sometimes they dropped if it wasn't windy. Now and then, from far away, I heard a truck laboring up Gap Hill. I could always hear Nancy's regular breathing in the bed beside me. In the woods at Crystal Flow Camp, there were no pears or corn, and my sister was far away.

On the last evening at camp, we gathered in the chapel. The colorful God's eyes we'd made from yarn and popsicle sticks dangled from the rafters. The counselors reminded us of all the fun we'd had during the week and gave out awards for the Bible Bee. Maple Cabin won, of course. Oak got the prize for volleyball. At the end of the festivities, Pastor Hershey, who had been around camp from time to time during the week, stood up and spoke: "We have had a blessed week together, and all of us leave better prepared to serve Jesus." I expected that to be the end of it, expected he'd go into the final prayer, but then he read out the names of the five campers who had been born again and accepted Christ as their personal Savior during the week. He said my name in front of everyone. He assured us he would inform the pastors of our various congregations of the important decision we had made. In the light of the chapel, the step I had taken suddenly felt more serious. Word would get out. I should have known that now I would be expected to join the church. It all went together. It wasn't just between me and Jesus and the other campers, and, of course, Glenn.

As soon as Mother learned I was born again, she took me to the covering store, where I chose the smallest prayer covering I could find among the many styles and sizes offered. "You're not getting one of those little things," she said. "You may as well wear a little doily." So I was stuck with a bigger one, but at least mine wasn't as big as hers. I couldn't believe I would need to go out into the world every day wearing a prayer covering.

When I returned to school a few weeks later, none of my friends mentioned my covering, and I often forgot it was perched there on my head. I'd be talking to someone, and I'd realize they weren't meeting my eyes but looking at my covering. Eventually, it didn't seem they noticed it at all, and I got more used to it too. I thought I should feel different inside, with the relief of being born again, but I didn't.

I started instruction class in preparation for being baptized, going to church for an hour every week to sit with the minister as he explained the rules and doctrines of the Mennonite Church to me and the two other teenagers joining the church at the same time. He spent a lot of time on the "Christian Life and Conduct" chapter in the instruction book, reviewing all the things we could *not* do—pretty much anything that sounded like fun—things like going to movies, playing cards, watching television, dancing. They were things I had never been allowed to do anyway, even before I was born again. The minister was intent we learn the order of God's plan. God is the head of all, then Jesus, then man and, lastly, woman. Somehow, in a way I didn't quite understand, the instruction book explained that wearing a prayer covering was a reminder of that order. The Bible verse that was used to positively mandate the importance of wearing the prayer covering was: "Every woman who prays or prophesies with her head uncovered dishonors her head." I guess it didn't make any difference that I didn't plan to prophesy in school. I needed to wear the covering anyway.

I had so many questions I wanted to ask the minister, but there was little opportunity for discussion, only for repeating what we had heard. At times I wanted to argue, but I listened and tried to believe, tried to rest in the assurance I was now safely in the fold and could look forward to eternity in heaven. Maybe understanding would happen for me later.

I should have considered that going through the motions may have counted for nothing, but I did it nonetheless. If the bishop doubted that I took seriously my promises to follow the doctrines of the Mennonite Church as he baptized me, he gave no indication. As I knelt in front of him wearing the modest cape dress Mother had made for me, I thought I was sincere. I wanted to believe, or at least thought I did.

# On Foot-Washing Sunday

Every Sunday we drove a half hour to a small Mennonite mission. The church we'd attended when I was younger was five minutes away, and we drove by a few other Mennonite churches on our way to the mission, but that particular mission was where we needed to go, because my parents had been called. The drive over twisting country roads sometimes made me carsick.

I didn't know what it meant that my parents felt "called" to go off to that mission. To me it felt pretty much like the people in charge at our regular church asked my parents to do it, and they couldn't say no. I'm sure they prayed about it, but the calling part, I think, happened as soon as they were asked and didn't have much to do with the Holy Spirit. They said they wanted to show Jesus's love to the people who lived near the little church on top of the hill. We, their children, went along to worship with people who in every other area of our lives we avoided. We went to school with some of them but would never have been their friends. At school I didn't let on I knew them.

Neither before nor after I joined the church did I have any interest in bringing Jesus to the mountain people who lived near the mission. But off we went each Sunday and usually on Wednesday, past trailers and rundown shacks guarded by scrawny barking dogs, past lawns strewn with discarded appliances and rusted cars. I had no interest in getting to know these people better. Although we would never have said or done anything to them directly, my siblings and I often laughed about them behind their backs, doing imitations and making up cruel nicknames. If we were intended to be part of the mission to show Jesus's love to the "least of these," we did not do our share.

I don't remember if I actually said mean things or laughed when my brothers did their impressions. I may have simply ignored them. I know I never said anything like "That's mean, what you're saying. How do you think it would be for you if you didn't have indoor plumbing?" I never suggested we invite some of the mountain kids home one Sunday afternoon and help them with their homework so they could do better in school. Most of them were in the lowest classes and dropped out long before graduation. I would never have considered speaking to them at school. At the church fellowship meals every few months, I stayed as far away from them as I could. If any of them had brought food to share, which they never did, I wouldn't have gone near it.

After I was born again and accepted Christ as my personal Savior, it was at that mission church where I was baptized and officially received into the fellowship . . . thus able to take Communion, an ordinance that felt part privilege and part responsibility. I didn't know how it would feel to participate.

I had been at church when Communion took place twice a year for as long as I could remember, first sitting next to Mother and, when I was older, among my peers, but never able to take part until I joined the church. It always felt like an interminable and mysterious production. First there was the bishop's long sermon, the mournful songs. Then the bishop passed the plate of stacked bread cubes, and I'd wait while everyone did their prayerful chewing. After the bread, the cup was passed, and each member took a sip of grape juice. No part of it seemed more mysterious than when people disappeared into the back room for foot washing, an important part of the service.

Communion-related activities went on for at least a week, starting with Counsel Meeting, to make sure everyone in the church community was at peace with themselves and each other. Not many young church members attended Counsel Meeting, the assumption, perhaps, that we wouldn't know what peace was. I never quite knew how Counsel

Meeting worked. My parents sometimes came home discussing disagreements among church members about spending money on a new roof or redoing the restrooms. It didn't make sense to me. What did peace have to do with a new roof?

Preparatory service happened the day before Communion. The few times I went, it felt a lot like Communion but without the bread and grape juice. The scriptures sounded the same, reminders of the Last Supper and Jesus's suffering. There was no shortage of mournful hymns for both preparatory service and Communion.

The first time I took Communion, after I was baptized, it wasn't at all what I expected. I knew the bread and juice were not magically turned into something else. But still. The bread tasted pretty much like store-bought white bread to me, and the grape juice? To be honest, the grape juice Mother canned from the grapes growing on the arbor along our back walk tasted better, even if it wasn't sanctified. For all the praying over it, I had expected something different. Had the bishop done something wrong? Had I? And that little sip of juice was not enough to wash down the bread, which clumped up at the top of my throat and didn't feel sacred at all. I knew I was supposed to be thinking of Jesus shedding his blood for me, not notice that the grape juice tasted watered-down. I wondered if there was something wrong with me.

I didn't like drinking grape juice from the same cup as everyone else. At home, when we were working in the field, we all drank ice water from the same Mason jar. But that was different. We were all family. I knew the people at church were supposed to feel like family too, the way everyone called each other brother and sister, but they didn't really feel that way. Not to me anyway.

It was the second time I had taken Communion. After the bishop finished the Bible readings about the Last Supper and Crucifixion, we shared bread and grape juice and sang, "There is a fountain filled with blood, drawn from Emmanuel's veins, and sinners plunged beneath that flood lose all their guilty stains." I didn't think about the disturbing images in the words I was singing so heartily . . . the idea of a whole fountain filled with blood. I didn't consider my guilty stains, what they were or whether I had, indeed, lost them. I did not think about sins I had not yet even heard of. Back then I just sang along.

The worst of the service was yet to come. Foot washing. Because Jesus had washed the disciples' feet the night before he was crucified and commanded all his followers to do the same, foot washing had become a sacred part of the Communion service. It was mortifying. Any symbolism of humility and service was lost on me, as, I suspect, it was on most teenagers. Maybe on some adults too.

Years later I would be moved when I heard news reports of Pope Francis washing the feet of prisoners, or read of couples who incorporated foot washing into their marriage ceremonies. In my teenage zeal to question and challenge, how could I have so missed the poignant significance of that simple and compassionate gesture?

The first time I had participated in Communion, the bishop's wife had washed my feet, and I hers. She did it carefully, gently, splashing water over every part of my feet, then wrapping each of them in a towel and drying them thoroughly. I was embarrassed and self-conscious when it was my turn to wash her feet, but I tried to do it the way she had. It felt strange touching someone's feet so gently. I didn't even know her. When we were finished, she embraced and kissed me. The "holy kiss," it was called, and I was even more embarrassed. I had never imagined that's how foot washing in the back room worked. It seemed even more outrageous to think about the men in their back room washing each other's feet and giving each other holy kisses. I thought of asking my older brothers how they felt about it, but I never did.

When I anticipated my second Communion, the thing I dreaded most was foot washing, even more than everyone drinking from the same cup. I knew I probably wouldn't get paired with the bishop's wife again. That happened only the first time after you were baptized so she could show you how it was done.

After the bishop read the passage about Jesus washing his disciples' feet, the bishop's wife worked her way back down the rows of women, first the older women sitting in front, dressed in somber dark dresses, as if it were a funeral. She directed who should go next into the back room, in pairs of two. There was probably no one in the congregation that Sunday whose feet I would less like to wash than Sarah's, and that was who the bishop's wife chose for me.

Sarah was an older, almost blind woman, who smelled of coal oil, a body needing bathing and clothes needing laundering. At the direction of the bishop's wife, who touched her arm and helped her up, Sarah shuffled into the back room. The bishop's wife motioned for me to follow. In that room, where coats were hung, two white basins filled with water sat on the floor in front of a wooden bench, a stack of towels in the corner. Feeling for the end of the bench, Sarah sat down. With shaking hands, she untied her shoes, unfastened and peeled down her stockings. I knelt down and slid the basin of lukewarm water under her feet. I tried not to look at her lumpy bunions, the calluses, her black toenail. Doing one foot at a time, I splashed the water over and around, trying not to touch her. I grabbed a towel and dried her feet quickly, not gently and thoroughly as the bishop's wife had done with me.

When I finished, I stood up and mumbled, "God bless you, Sarah," as we were supposed to. I glanced around. Since no one was watching, I did not embrace or kiss her. Because Sarah could not bend down or see to wash my feet, I did not take off my shoes and stockings but hurried back to where I'd been sitting, leaving her, no doubt, to struggle pulling on her stockings over still-damp feet, standing up, and feeling her way back to her bench.

I might have tried to soothe Sarah's tired feet, to dry them more carefully, to help her on with her stockings. I might have helped her up and led her to her seat, said "God bless you, sister," and meant it. But I didn't.

On the drive home from church, everyone in the car was quiet. After the long service, we were all hungry. Anticipating that, Mother had planned a meal she could get on the table quickly. She had set the oven to come on while we were gone to bake the ham and scalloped potatoes.

Although I had scarcely touched Sarah's feet, I scrubbed my hands with soap and hot water as soon as we got home, before I set the table.

"Who did you wash with today?" Mother asked, emptying the jar of applesauce into a bowl.

"Sarah." It made me feel grownup that she asked me about it.

"Poor Sarah," she said. "I wish there was more we could do for her."

"Yeah," I said. I didn't tell her I hadn't done what little I could, let alone more. I hadn't given it a thought.

Of all the Bible verses I'd learned when I was growing up, I would have said I liked the ones about serving "the least of these," the idea that Jesus comes to us in the form of the hungry, the needy, those vulnerable in every way. Maybe the reason I liked it when preachers chose those verses was because there was little they could do to interpret the verses in a way that would inspire a sermon about how women should dress or behave, a far too common theme, it seemed. Years later, I was drawn to the Quakers because of their belief that there is a spark of the divine in each of us, and we live to find it in ourselves and each other. Offered the opportunity to serve one of the least of these on that long-ago foot-washing Sunday, I know I might have done so much better.

When I think back on that experience, I cannot believe that my teenage self-consciousness inspired such an arrogant lack of compassion. It may not have made any difference for Sarah had I been kinder to her—she would still have been almost blind, still needed to return to her dark, cramped house. But it might have made her feel better in that moment to know that someone cared enough to show her some small kindness.

# One of the Plain Girls

I needed a part-time job. I'd been babysitting for neighbors, but I couldn't make much money from that. Sometimes they didn't pay me but gave me something instead—stockings, candy bars, a pack of underwear, something they'd picked up while they were shopping. I would rather have had money, but Mother said I should be grateful for whatever they gave me.

"You should apply at Plain and Fancy," my friend Marie said to me one morning after church. "Mrs. Flory likes to hire plain girls."

As much as I didn't see myself as a plain girl, I wanted a job, and Plain and Fancy, unlike a lot of the local businesses that catered to tourists, was closed on Sunday. My parents would agree to a job like that. They wouldn't have given me permission to take a job requiring me to work on Sunday. They didn't think any business should be open on Sunday. We observed it as a day of rest, doing only the things needing to be done, like feeding and milking cows, taking care of the chickens, and gathering eggs.

After we all returned from church and ate dinner, Sunday was the day to set up croquet wickets in the front yard and play all afternoon—even Mother played—or string a net between the trees and play volleyball. We played board games or read. Relatives often visited on Sunday, or we went to visit them. Hoes and rakes and shovels sat idle, and we would not have considered working in the fields on Sunday.

My parents didn't hesitate to give me permission to apply to work at Plain and Fancy. I had recently gotten my driver's license, and they said I could drive to work in the new red Ford Econoline truck if no one else needed it. If we had outside jobs in our family, we were expected to give most of what we earned to our parents, keeping only part of it for saving or spending. I never thought to question that practice. It made sense we should all contribute to household expenses, since we were living at home. I was surprised when I learned from friends who had jobs that they got to keep all their money and didn't even need to buy their own clothes. Although I had to give most of the money I earned to my parents, I'd still have more than I did before.

Plain and Fancy was developed and owned by a Mennonite family and had opened a few years before, the name of the business echoing the title of a Broadway musical that had recently opened, a show no good Mennonite would have ever gone to see. Plain and Fancy included a family-style restaurant, a gift shop, and the farmhouse set up to look like a typical Amish home. Mrs. Flory hired me the same day I filled out the application. Apparently I was plain enough for her, but I wasn't as plain as she was. She wore the same style dress as my mother and other adult women in the church—long, buttonless, shapeless dresses in either solid colors or muted prints. All of them featured an extra piece over the bodice, the part called the cape. I could wear skirts and blouses, as long as I was dressed modestly.

Mrs. Flory explained that my main job would be to guide tours through the simulated Amish farmhouse. Between tours I'd work in the adjacent gift shop. While I was in school, I'd be scheduled to work a few weekdays after school and on Saturdays. In the summer I'd work full time. I would finally be able to buy some of my own clothes and save money for college.

One day after school I went for training. It was almost closing time, and there weren't many tourists. I went along with Mrs. Flory as she guided the tour. She directed the group as we moved from the kitchen, the living room, a parlor set up for church, and bedrooms upstairs with simple handmade furniture, colorful quilts, and, hanging on pegs from the wall, samples of the clothing members of the Amish family might wear. The tourists in the group asked a couple of questions but didn't seem to care much about what Mrs. Flory was saying, and she didn't make any of it sound very interesting. I took a few notes.

After observing one more tour, I told Mrs. Flory I felt ready to guide tours on my own. It was a Saturday, and, when I arrived for work, tourists from the buses were already wandering about the grounds. The first tour was mine. I wasn't used to talking in front of people I didn't know, not even people I did know. I was nervous. Twelve people crowded into the Amish kitchen around the large table.

"An Amish family spends much of their time in the kitchen," I said, "where they do all of their cooking, canning, and baking, and where they gather for meals. They have no electricity, so cooking and baking are done with a cook stove. They burn coal or wood. In summer they might use propane. Lighting is provided by coal oil or gas lamps." I pointed out the lamp hanging over the table. Mrs. Flory had told me it couldn't be lit because of fire regulations. My voice felt shaky, but if it quivered when I talked, no one seemed to notice. My mouth felt dry, but still I seemed to have too much saliva and wasn't sure when to swallow.

"By fall, most Amish pantries are filled with food for the winter." I pointed to the open pantry door, where you could see a dozen or more canning jars on the shelves—peaches, applesauce, red beets, pickles.

One of the tourist women glanced in the door and said to her children, "Look at all those canned things," in a tone making it sound like those few puny jars were a big deal. They didn't look like much to me, not compared to the hundreds of jars on our canning shelves, but maybe the tourist woman didn't have a pantry, or her children were used to cans rather than jars.

I knew the basics about the Amish. I had gone to school with Amish kids for the elementary grades, but they dropped out in eighth grade to stay home and help on their farms. They were our neighbors but mostly stayed to themselves. I didn't know much about their history. I knew that back in the Old Country, Mennonites and Amish were all part of a group called the Anabaptists. I wasn't sure why they separated or when. I took it for granted that Amish drove only horses and buggies and didn't have electricity or telephones in their homes, but I had never thought about why. It was simply the way they lived. They were part of the landscape, like silos and white barns and tidy flower beds.

Sometimes one of the tourists asked me a question I wasn't sure how to answer. A man, usually. "How do the Amish and Mennonites fit into the Protestant Reformation?" one of them might ask.

"They were a part of it," I'd say, having little idea what I was talking about, moving the group on to the next room, and hoping there would be no follow-up question. "The Amish and Mennonites were originally part of the same group," I explained as the tourists collected in the room set up for Amish church, with row after row of backless benches.

"Why did they split?" someone would often ask.

"The Mennonites were too progressive," I'd say, which I was pretty sure was true, since we had cars and phones and electricity. It almost always got a laugh from someone.

When there was a slow time, with no tourists waiting to go through the house, I'd look at the books on the racks in the gift shop, *Getting to Know the Amish* and *Mennonite Life*. I read them to learn history and dates, and tried to find answers for the questions that challenged me. I checked the encyclopedias in the school library, and I asked Mother. By the end of the second or third week, I was sure I knew more than Mrs. Flory ever did.

I hated it when teenagers were in the group. If they asked questions, they were almost always focused on clothing or what teenagers did for fun. Their questions made me feel like I had to defend the Amish and Mennonite teenagers, and I usually didn't feel like it.

"The Amish women's dresses have no buttons," I explained, pointing to the dress hanging on the peg in the master bedroom upstairs, "and are always solid colors."

"How come you're wearing something different?" one girl asked. "Your cap is totally different." It was as if she thought this was a theme park, and I'd put on the wrong costume to come to work.

"Oh, I'm not Amish," I said, mortified she might have thought I was that plain and unworldly. It was uncomfortable when questions focused on me, as if I was somehow part of the spectacle they had come to see.

"How does it feel, all these people coming to gawk at you all the time?" one woman asked. "Oh, no," I wanted to say. "They're here to see the Amish, not me." How could the tourists think I was part of the quaint backward life they had come to witness? I had not dropped out of school after eighth grade to stay home and work on the farm. I planned to go to college. To the tourists, I was of interest because they thought I was one of the "plain people." Couldn't they tell there was so much more to me? I was a woman of the world!

I had taken the train to New York City a few weeks earlier to visit my sister Grace, who was living and working there. She met me at Penn Station, and I was excited to see her. Her life in New York, living with a few other Mennonite girls, working as a dietician in a big hospital— all of it sounded exciting to me. The first thing she said to me when she saw me coming up the stairs at the station was "Take off that covering. People don't wear them up here." I felt like I had embarrassed her. I went into the rest room, quickly unpinned it, folded it, and put it in my purse. I didn't wear it for the rest of the weekend, not to the Bronx Zoo or to Radio City Music Hall, or to go to the top of the Empire State Building. It felt good not wearing a covering. We went shopping, and I bought New York City clothes—a blouse and skirt and sweater— with some of my work money. Grace's Mennonite roommates were fun, and none of them wore coverings either. I didn't put mine back on until I was on the train going home, and the conductor announced, "Next stop Lancaster." I took the covering out of my purse, crouched down in my seat, and pinned it back in place.

When I visited New York, I might have been walking down streets in some of the tourists' neighborhoods. Who knows? They might have walked right by me and not have known I was one of the plain girls.

Sometimes a tourist would try to embarrass me. "Seems like a lot of them have big families," he'd say.

"That's true," I said.

"I guess those farmers don't spend all their time working in the fields," he'd say, laughing, looking at the others in the group, as if only *they* would understand what he meant. Of course, I didn't say anything in response. I hoped no one asked me how many were in my family. I could have said anything, but I wouldn't have. I would have told them there were twelve children, and I was the tenth. I didn't want to think about my parents that way. What child does? I'd never seen my parents so much as hold hands.

After I started reading more about Mennonite and Amish history, I was reminded of all the terrible things that had happened to some of them in Europe in the sixteenth and seventeenth centuries, and they never fought back. They were burned at the stake or hanged, and all they did in response was sing or pray. It wasn't that I felt proud of them for how they behaved. Not exactly. But those early Mennonites weren't hurting anyone, just thinking a little differently, not accepting the way things were. Maybe that's all it took to be dangerous to the people in charge. How could anyone keep torturing someone who was singing or praying? Thousands of those early Mennonites were burned or drowned. I didn't tell those stories to the tourists, because there were often children in the group. You didn't bring your kids to Amish country to scare them with stories about people being tortured and killed.

Although I seldom found a place to include it in the tour, unless someone specifically asked how it happened that the Amish and Mennonites came to settle in Pennsylvania, one of my favorite parts of the history was about William Penn inviting people from all over Europe who were being persecuted. He said they could come to Pennsylvania but needed to treat the Indians right, since they were here first. I didn't know how that part worked, but I was pretty sure the Mennonites didn't kill the Native Americans who'd been living in eastern Pennsylvania all along. We must have been living on their land, since we sometimes found Indian arrowheads when we plowed the fields. My brother Charles had collected a whole box of them. I didn't know how it happened that the Mennonites had gotten their land. Someone must have told them they had to sell it and made them leave. I hoped it wasn't my ancestors.

For the fifteen or twenty minutes it took to direct the tours through the Amish farmhouse, everyone listened to me. As I learned more, I added to the stories, felt more sure of myself, and had better answers to the questions. I didn't know what the tourists were thinking as they stood listening, but it felt like my words held them. When I said, "Move on to the next room," they did. I felt like more than just one of the plain girls; I felt like a girl who knew what she was talking about. On the rare occasions one of the tourists gave me a tip, I'd hold onto it until I could slip it into my purse under the desk in the gift shop. I only needed to give my paycheck to my parents. They hadn't said anything about tips.

We had a great time, the other plain girls and I, working together at Plain and Fancy, especially on the days Mrs. Flory wasn't in the gift shop making us feel like plain girls weren't supposed to have fun. We made up categories for the tourists who came through the house— the chatty ones, the overbearing, the know-it-alls, the senior citizens, the curious locals. When we saw them walk up the path toward the entrance, we tried to predict their types and anticipate who might be annoying on the tour. Mrs. Flory heard us talking and laughing one day and told us we shouldn't make fun of the customers, which we weren't really. We were enjoying ourselves. They were looking at us. Why couldn't we look at them?

It wasn't unusual at the end of a tour for one of the tourist mothers to stay behind and say something like "All those lovely farms, parents teaching their children good values, growing their own food, helping each other. Such a beautiful way of life." Of course, she didn't know all of it, but I could see her point about the positive things. I knew the Bible warned "Pride goeth before a fall," but, in those moments, I sometimes felt almost proud I was part of that way of life . . . until I remembered how eager I was to get away as soon as I could.

# Considering Lilies
## of the Field

Mother kept diaries for eighty years, from 1920 to 2000, and I have no reason to doubt the accuracy of her record-keeping. When she noted that on a January day in 1944, she dressed 23 chickens, I believe it. In May of that year, she planted 500 strawberry plants, and on March 29, 1953, she gathered 304 eggs. I take no issue with her numbers; however, when she reported in her entry in April 1964, "Mary Alice is in a rage about going to a movie with the Buckwalters and went without our consent," I questioned it.

I didn't question that I actually went to the movie. I did. And I went without permission. How could I forget that? It's the *rage* I question. I have no idea what my teenage rage would have looked like. I had no role model for rage. In our family we did not rage or overtly express many emotions at all. On Gapview Farm we kept a cap on our feelings. We had too much to do. The chaos *rage* might have produced was a luxury we could not afford. The conversation must have started when I got home from school.

"I want to go to a movie with Suzanne this evening," I said.

"You know we don't go to movies," Mother said, stirring the browned butter into the noodles, not even glancing up.

"But it's a good movie. About building a chapel."

"It doesn't matter what it's about. We don't go to movies."

"That doesn't make any sense. I mean, the title of the movie is *Lilies of the Field*. It's from a Bible verse." I knew better than to use that argument.

It was a movie, after all. It didn't matter what it was about or what it was called. Mother dropped it. She knew there was no future in arguing with me. She often said to me, "You'll argue till you're blue in the face." I'm sure I did, but arguing was different from raging. Maybe it looked the same to her. Why did I think I could wear her down with reason? I should have known if church rules were involved, reason and common sense were useless.

After supper I dried the dishes and then watched out the front window until I saw the Buckwalter's car creeping up the lane. Mother was sitting in her rocking chair darning socks. I left without saying a word. No one stopped me.

Growing up, all those times I sat in Mennonite Sunday school, none of the Ten Commandments was clearer or drilled into our memories more routinely than "Honor thy father and thy mother." As if it wasn't clear enough from the Old Testament, it was repeated in the New Testament, "Children, obey your parents that your days might be long upon the earth." It felt important and absolute, with no wiggle room. I had usually taken it seriously.

Going to that movie was the first time I recall doing anything so blatantly rebellious and disobedient. No movie I've seen since has made such a lasting impression. The problem with movies was more than the edification question that was the gold standard for any book, game, or amusement we exposed ourselves to. Edification, as nearly as I could tell, had to do with being of value, either teaching you something or making you a better person.

"Is that book edifying?" Mother would ask when in junior high I returned from the bookmobile with a Betty Cavanna book. She asked it as if it were a separate Dewey Decimal classification, with a few shelves of books I should limit myself to. I always said, "Yes," and she didn't have time to read *Going on Sixteen* or *A Girl Can Dream* to pass her own judgment before I needed to return the books. In truth, she did not consider most fiction edifying, and I would certainly have been hard-pressed to make a case for the Betty Cavanna books I read voraciously for a couple summers. Maybe they were edifying, teaching me as they did about a world outside my reach, the teenage characters involved with doing things I could only imagine.

The problem with movies went beyond edification. Simply because it *was* a movie, there was no way for it to be edifying, no matter what its subject. Although I couldn't imagine any of our Mennonite preachers ever having been to a movie, they warned us we would not want to be in a movie theater when the Lord returned. I thought an all-knowing God might know the difference between a worthwhile movie and one with too much sex, violence, or swearing, but the theater itself was a problem. Satan lured you in with movies that might seem harmless. After you got comfortable in the theater, before you knew it, the preachers might have warned, you'd be watching people wearing hardly any clothes, and having sex and killing people and smoking and drinking and swearing. You had to look at the whole picture.

My friend Sherry had already seen *Lilies of the Field*.

"It's a great movie," she said, "and Sidney Poitier looks good. You should hear his accent."

"Anything bad at all?" I asked.

"Are you kidding? It's a bunch of nuns. There's not even a swear word."

We went into the theater, the Buckwalters and I, and the lights went down. The movie started, and Sidney Poitier arrived in some remote town, looking as good as Sherry had promised he would, and asked the nuns for water for his overheating car. One thing led to another, and he decided to stay for a while. He started building a chapel for the nuns. I loved the way he said "chapel," like it was spelled "shapel." He taught the nuns to speak English, but I could understand a lot of what they were saying when they spoke German. How can you say it's not edifying, practicing the foreign language you're studying in school? The ending was beautiful, the nuns and Sidney Poitier singing "Amen" together, and you could hear them singing together even after he got in his car and drove away. In that dark theater, as the gentle film drew me in, and I watched Sidney Poitier build the chapel, I didn't give the Second Coming a second thought.

We drove home after the movie, Suzanne and her mother and sister and I, all singing "Amen" together as loud as we could. After they dropped me off and I sneaked quietly up to my room through the dark house, the song echoed in my head as I fell asleep. I had disobeyed my parents and gone to a movie. I was sure there would be consequences, but I was grateful the Second Coming had not happened while I was in the theater with no chance to repent. The movie was so good, I couldn't think about it being sinful. I must have said my prayers before I went to bed. I doubt I asked forgiveness for seeing the movie—it did not seem to be a thing needing forgiveness. I may have mentioned my disobedience.

Between spoons full of cereal the next morning, I said to Mother, "The movie was really good," as if that would make a difference. "The nuns needed a church, and this black guy comes by, and he built it for them. They never lost faith, and, in the end, the whole town gets involved, everyone working together. It was like an Amish barn raising."

She didn't say anything, stirring the dough in the mixing bowl. There was a big difference, I knew. How could anything be like an Amish barn raising if nuns were involved? Nuns were Catholics. Where to start? I knew that arguing the film's merits by mentioning the nuns wasn't going to help my case, but how could I explain Lilies of the Field without mentioning nuns? They were a main part of it.

On the whole, Mennonites in our community were apolitical, choosing not to vote, no doubt based on the argument that a pacifist could not vote for the commander in chief of the military. In spite of that, some church members were moved to abandon the nonvoting practice when John F. Kennedy ran for president. A Catholic running for office was enough to send people to the polls who had never voted before. When I was growing up, I often heard about the "Catholic problem," with ministers warning about it from the pulpit. The Catholics/Pope/ Antichrist, with their Virgin Mary–worshipping ways, were on a mission to take over the United States, and a Catholic president would only be the beginning. It wouldn't be long till they'd want us all to be worshipping the Virgin Mary and graven images. I would later learn that the only time Daddy may have voted was when Al Smith, a Catholic, was running in the 1920s. As far as I know, Mother never voted, but both she and Daddy understood the "Catholic problem." The nuns in *Lilies of the Field* were part of the same outfit. I didn't know much about Catholics, but the way I understood it back then, their hell was a place you could work or pay your way out of. You could sin recklessly, and priests would explain to you how to make all your sins go away.

Rita, a friend from school, was the only Catholic I knew, but being Catholic was not her only problem. She and her family lived over the Rising Sun Tavern, which her father managed, and it was the only bar in town. "That hellhole" my father sometimes called it when we drove by. I knew better than to ask to visit Rita, although she and her family seemed nice enough. Just like the nuns in the movie.

I finished eating my cereal but still hadn't heard anything about punishment. Not that we often had punishment, or deserved it. There was the time Sanford had to go to his room without supper when he stayed for the soccer playoff game without permission. It wasn't much of a punishment, since Nancy and I took food to him in his room, but it was immediate and dramatic. Surely something should happen to me for going to the movie without permission, but what could you do to an almost eighteen-year-old? If I didn't get to drive the car or truck to work, someone would have to take me. And I often had to stay after school for yearbook meetings. I had responsibilities.

The most memorable and effective discipline I had ever received was the time I talked back to my mother about a chore I didn't want to do—something about dishes, no doubt. Mother said, "All right then. We'll wear the old things out first," and I had to sit and watch her wash and dry the dishes all by herself. The dishes were stacked high, and it took her a long time. She looked old and tired as she bent over the sink. I felt awful . . . and never again complained about a chore.

Soon I would graduate from high school. When you were almost an adult, maybe there was a higher authority to answer to than parents. Ordinary consequences paled in comparison to the threat of hellfire. I almost wished Mother would come up with something.

I was, from all appearances, a good girl. I attended church every week, as was expected, and could pretty convincingly answer any questions the Sunday school teacher might ask. I had been baptized and joined the church, but deep down I didn't feel any different. I was supposed to be "born again," but I honestly wasn't sure what that meant. I hadn't felt sinful before and did not feel my sins had been washed away afterward. I wondered if I had done it wrong. I had gone through the right motions, and it seemed to make my parents happy, but it also seemed I should feel different.

In school, I was not at the top of my class but close enough, and I never presented any behavior problems. If I was in the hall between classes, no monitor asked me for a pass, assuming I was on some sort of important business, certainly not causing trouble. The principal of the high school was briefly upset about a critical editorial I had written in the school newspaper, *The Pioneer*, about the lack of vocational opportunities for students not interested in college or farming, but I'm sure the teacher who sponsored the newspaper got in more trouble than I did.

I knew being mostly good might count for nothing. I had heard more than one preacher warn that Satan would lull you into believing that being good or doing good would be enough to get you into heaven, but if you weren't born again, none of it would help. I feared I was one of those people who thought good works would save me.

Some of the church rules were hard for me to accept, I'll admit. Many of them seemed arbitrary, and I questioned them, particularly the oppressive specifics about women's dress and grooming. Many of them focused on modesty, a concept, as I understood it, having to do with how much flesh a woman left exposed. Since the Bible was called "The Word of God," I somehow gave God credit for the rules. I thought some of my arguments around the inconsistencies of church rules were brilliant, things like "How could the Bible say television is wrong when it hadn't even been invented back in the day?" or "If it's bad to wear red, why did God create geraniums?" or "There's nowhere in the Bible where lipstick is mentioned." Mother was often silent in the face of such challenges, which I took as proving the strength of my arguments.

It didn't occur to me that the church rules came from preachers and bishops, regular men chosen to be ministers, and not directly from God. As it began to dawn on me that the men in the church had a big role in making the rules, I sometimes thought, but would never have said, "Why should I listen to a bunch of farmers?" I knew that's what most of the bishops and preachers were. At that time they had little training or education and were chosen in a mysterious and suspenseful ritual called "the lot." The congregation would choose a few men to be considered for minister. At a somber service, those men would sit at the front of the church. Each would choose a Bible from those spread out on a table in front of the pulpit, one for each candidate. In only one was a slip of paper indicating they had been the one chosen by God to be ordained.

The process was particularly stressful for the candidates' families. Daddy was once in "the lot," and Mother, after it was all done, admitted she had offered some prayers that God might see his way clear to choose someone else. We were all relieved when the slip of paper had not appeared in Daddy's Bible. Although a good man, he was not preacher material. I would not have wanted to criticize God, but it was hard for me to understand why some of the men were chosen. I seldom stopped to consider how seriously they took their callings or to give them credit for doing their best with very little training.

As much as I wanted to believe in a God who could see into a darkened theater and discern the worth of individual movies rather than damn them all, that thought was also disquieting. Such an all-knowing God could also see into my soul and know what a sham I was, with all my doubts and questions. Maybe I didn't want a God who could see into the darkness after all.

# It's Only Fair

I had waited as long as I could. The college application was lying upstairs on my desk, and the deadline was approaching. I needed a parent's signature, and it was time to talk to them about it. Abe, my oldest brother, said I could live with him and his family to help out with their kids and cut down on my expenses. At least two colleges were within commuting distance of his house.

In the kitchen, the smell of liver and onions had already faded, and all that remained was the faint, fatty smell of the lye soap Mother used to wash dishes. I had dried all the dishes and stacked the last of the everyday plates in the cupboard.

I had to catch my parents quickly, before Daddy, who was looking through the mail, fell asleep in his rocking chair reading *The Farm Journal* or *Christian Living*, before Mother sat down in her chair, soaking her feet in a tub of warm water with Epsom salts while she mended. She was already sorting through a stack of worn socks. I hung the damp dish towel on the rack at the end of the cupboard and cleared my throat.

"There's something I need to talk to both of you about," I said.

"Sounds serious," Daddy said.

They sat down at the table, and I sat opposite them, my hands in front of me on the flowered oilcloth. It felt odd not having them at their places on either end, where they sat for every meal. In the quiet I could hear the quivering buzz of the fluorescent light and, in the distance, the faint sound of Sanford bouncing the basketball. Dale had already driven off in his new Corvair to go to what he called "Fire Meeting." The volunteer firemen hung out at the firehouse, played cards or pool, waiting, in case there was a fire. I don't know where Nancy was, probably reading somewhere. And that was all the family left at home. There had been twelve of us, and now there were only four.

"I need you to sign my college application," I said. "It's time to send it in."

"You weren't thinking of going right away, were you?" Daddy said.

"I want to go in the fall. I don't see any point in waiting. In a few months I'll graduate, and everyone at school says I'm college material."

"I think you know that's not how we do it in this family. A lot of the older ones were college material too, but they waited a few years, worked and saved up money, then went when they were sure it's what they wanted."

"But I'm already sure it's what I want. I don't see any point in working at some stupid job while I save up money to go later. I can get scholarships, borrow money." I tried to keep my voice calm, but I could feel it trembling.

"Say you want to get married in a few years," Daddy said. "A man doesn't want a woman who brings along a whole lot of debt. Plus, all that education to end up keeping house. It'd be a waste."

What he didn't say, but I had heard it before, was that if a woman got too educated, she'd end up being an "unclaimed blessing." Mother insisted on using that term rather than "spinster" or "old maid," which she thought disrespectful. I had not given much thought to getting married, nor did I aspire to be an "unclaimed blessing." I had not dated, nor thought much about it. I could deal with all of that later.

"I won't end up just keeping house. I plan to work, teach if I can."

"When your sister Rhoda was your age, she stayed home and helped with the little ones. I don't know what your mother would have done without her."

"She sure was a big help," Mother said, nodding toward Daddy.

I was tired hearing about "when Rhoda was your age." To believe our parents, my oldest sister had never done anything but what she was

asked, never talked back, never questioned their opinion, never challenged any of the church rules. She had set an impossibly high bar.
Rhoda was almost twenty years older than I was and had left home
shortly after I was born. Her oldest children were only a few years
younger than I. It seemed to me I was an aunt for as long as I could
remember.

"Times have changed since Rhoda was my age," I said. "Most people
now go to college right out of high school."

"We aren't most people," Daddy said. "I think you know that."

I should have. Mennonites worked hard not to be "most people,"
not to be of this world. One of the Bible verses we were taught was
"Come out from among them, and be ye separate." Whoever wrote
that clearly had no idea how it felt to be a teenager and want to fit in. In
the Old World, people had died for their beliefs, and all through history
Mennonites had done what they could so that things never changed. It
seemed to me the people in charge wanted us to live as our ancestors
had. Mother wore the same style clothes her mother and grandmother
had worn; we had no television or radio. Except for driving cars and
using tractors rather than horses for farming, it seemed to me that Mennonites tried to live much like those who'd come from Switzerland in
the early eighteenth century. The "times have changed" argument was
not going to help my case.

"If going to college is something you want so bad, you'll still want
it in a couple years," Daddy said. "And you won't be doing it because
everyone else is doing it. Charles is on his way to being a doctor, and
waiting didn't hurt him. Now he's learned to lay linoleum, and that's a
good skill to know. And look at Dale. He'll start at Penn State this year,
but helped out at home and worked a couple years. Now he knows
plumbing too."

"I think I've learned all I can about cleaning off tables at Plain and
Fancy Restaurant or guiding tours through the Amish Farmhouse."

Working at Plain and Fancy had been fun for a while, and I planned
to work there through the summer, but I was tired of being part of the
quaint population that tourists came to Lancaster County by the mil-
lions to see each year. I wanted to be a regular person.

Daddy said, "Your mother and I try to treat all you children the same. It's the only fair way to do things."

Mother picked up one of Daddy's socks from the mending stack, stretched it over the darning egg, and wove the heavy black thread back and forth over the hole in the heel.

I could think of no argument for "that's the way we do it in our family." It's not like I was asking for money. They wouldn't need to put out a penny, and any loan would be my debt. Who of my older brothers and sisters would care? Ike and Jim, my two brothers who were farmers, had plenty to do already. Rhoda had recently had her sixth child and had lots to keep up with. Milt had started a job teaching at a prep school on Long Island, and Grace was a dietician at a hospital in New York. I knew that Abe, who was a psychiatrist, or Charles, who was in medical school, would not care about me going to college. And Ray, who was by this time in a pre-veterinary program, had enough to do, studying textbooks about things I had never heard of. I couldn't imagine any of them giving much thought to their younger sister going to college right out of high school or, for that matter, giving much thought to me at all. About anything.

"I'll go crazy if I have to stay here helping on the farm and working at Plain and Fancy."

"Don't you think you're exaggerating a little?" Daddy said. "If you made it this long, I think you could survive a couple more years."

"That's because you're not the one who wants to go to college."

"You're making an awful big fuss out of a little thing, if you ask me," Daddy said. "A couple years from now college will still be there."

"What if I just do it?"

I wondered if there was a way to go to college whether or not they signed the form. Sure, it would be a bigger deal than the time I'd gone to the movies without permission, but what could they do? I mean, it was Abe's idea that I live with him and his family. He was a doctor, and, although my parents wouldn't have admitted it, they were proud of him and thought he was right about almost everything. If part of the plan was to help Abe and his wife, that should count for something. My parents wanted me to be useful, so how could they argue with me about helping out? We wouldn't need to focus on the college part. Abe was an adult; maybe he could sign the application. Feeling like he was on my side gave me courage I might not otherwise have had.

I got up from the bench and left the table. I wanted to slam the living room door on my way upstairs. I knew it would slam. I had heard Dale slam it one time after yelling at Ray, "You're not my boss." I thought it would feel good, slamming the door, but I was not a door-slamming kind of person. That's the thing of it; I'd tried to be a good daughter. I hadn't gotten my hair cut, although I wanted to, and I wore clothes that often embarrassed me. I tried not to offend my parents with skirts too short, sweaters too tight, or heels too high. I shook hands with all my relatives when they came to dinner, because I was supposed to. I even kissed a few of my great-aunts when they visited. I hated doing it, but Mother said it was important, so I did it.

I went upstairs to my room and threw myself down on the bed. I was angry and frustrated. Why did it need to be this hard? It wasn't like I was asking to join the Army or hitchhike cross-country. Go to college. Wouldn't most parents be thrilled?

Sure, being fair was a good thing. They didn't want to cause resentment in the family, but they took it too far. I mean, if Ike or Jim, my farmer brothers, had asked my parents if they could borrow money to buy a tractor, would my parents have said, "We can't do that unless we help all our children buy tractors?" What would I have done with a stupid tractor? Which proved my point. Sometimes it's not about fair. It's about different.

If I didn't aspire to be a housewife, the only two career choices I saw were teacher or nurse. I wouldn't have considered being a doctor, had never heard of a woman doctor. I knew being a nurse wasn't for me either. When my brother had his toe cut off by the lawn mower, I couldn't stand to look at it dangling all bloody. My sister Grace had been a nurse's aide, and, when she talked about it, it didn't sound like much fun to me, all that blood and vomit.

I wouldn't have made a good nurse, although I had helped my brother Ray caponize chickens for a few summers, and it was almost like I was his nurse assistant. I'd hold the chickens, wings in one hand, feet in the other while he made a small incision in their sides and pulled out clusters looking like little yellow beans. My brother said it was what would make them into roosters when they grew up. There was almost no blood, and my brother gave me part of the money he earned, but helping with caponizing was no career.

I wanted to be a teacher. Teachers had been important to me, and I wanted to be important like that for someone else. I had lots of role models. Maybe I could make a difference like my teachers had for me.

When I was eight, I'd said I wanted to be a book writer when I grew up. I didn't know any book writers and didn't spend much time thinking about where books came from, but I enjoyed folding paper. I'd save the expired calendar pages we tore off, fold them, and stitch them up the spine. I don't remember if I wrote my own stories or copied them. No matter. Being a book writer was not a real choice, because the main expectation in our family was that we do something to be "of use."

When I had calmed down, I went over to my desk and took out the college application. I had narrowed the possibilities down to one college, one of the two nearest Abe's house. I didn't have money for extra application fees. I was so naive that it would never have occurred to me to apply to more than one college to see who would give me the best financial aid. I assumed I'd get in wherever I applied.

I finished filling out the application, printing as neatly as I could. At the end, it asked for an essay about a person I admired. I considered the possibilities: older siblings who had dreamed big and gone to college, some of them with only a GED; teachers who had encouraged me over the years, who made me believe that I could make something of myself. And I put Mother on the list.

Mother. I did admire her, even though I was angry she had sat at the kitchen table darning holes in socks, saying almost nothing while Daddy said, "Your mother and I this, your mother and I that." I wasn't sure she agreed with all of what he said. I knew when she was young, she wanted to go to high school more than anything, but she had to stay home to help take care of her younger brothers and sisters. She wanted to graduate from high school and go on to nursing school. When I was in high school, she liked to read all the essays I wrote, the book reports, the term papers. She wasn't reading to help me improve them. She was reading to learn new things. She was interested in my assignments, my science projects—the rock collection, the insect collection, the heredity study I did of the family. She read my history textbook, even though she didn't need to. When I became interested in journalism, she supported my efforts to start a family newsletter, and she tried to go to every assembly or performance I or any of my siblings had a part in. She had a lot to do, and I admired her for taking the time. With all the children she'd raised, she didn't lose her temper or become impatient. Each day she did what needed to be done, efficiently and with good humor. And it wasn't like she did things just for the family. She was kind to everyone, especially to people like Sarah, those people she called "poor souls." She would not have treated Sarah the way I did if she had been chosen to wash her feet at Communion. She would have caressed her tired feet and helped her back to her seat. And she expected nothing in return for her kindness, not even gratitude. She took caring for "the least of these" seriously, and I admired her for it.

All it would have taken for her to be at the top of my "most admired" list at that moment, the one I wrote my essay about, would have been for her to say to Daddy, "You know, I think we could take a look at the way we've done things in the past, making everyone wait to go to college. It might make sense for Mary Alice to go right away if she wants it that bad. She's always been serious about school and learning. I don't think it would cause any problems at all with the other children." But she didn't say any of it.

There would come a time when I would wish I had written the essay about Mother, even if she didn't say all of what I might have wanted to hear that day. There was more than enough reason to warrant my admiration even without that.

I'm not sure why I perceived the life of a farm wife as one of thankless drudgery. Nothing could be further from the image my mother presented. She seemed to take joy in each day of hard work, of doing for her family. The rhythms of farm life and caring for her family seemed to sustain her physically, emotionally, and spiritually. I never once heard her complain about any of it. Even with that joyful role model, I was certain it was not the life for me.

I finished filling out the application, wrote the essay on Mrs. Conger, my high school English teacher, certainly another worthy choice. I'm sure I wrote about how she inspired me to have confidence, to believe in myself and my abilities. I was seventeen, and I suspect the essay was mostly about me. I hope I at least mentioned that she grew up in a remote town in the mountains of southwestern Virginia, a town not many people moved away from, especially not to go to college.

She had been my brother Dale's English teacher too, and he thought she was hard, which she was. She expected a lot, and it worked for me. The harder she pushed, the harder I worked. It's not like I didn't work hard for all my classes, because I did, but not like English. If I'd had time, I would have memorized every poem in the literature textbook, spent the whole summer reading all the books on the suggested reading list. Some of my classmates thought I was the teacher's pet, but I didn't care.

My parents liked Mrs. Conger too. Mother felt sorry for her that her family lived so far away and occasionally invited her for supper if she gave me a ride home after I stayed late to work on the newspaper. When Mrs. Conger's mother visited from Virginia, Mother invited her for a meal too, and everyone had a good time together.

I needed to stay after school to work on the newspaper the day after I'd had the talk with my parents. I worked at a table in the corner of Mrs. Conger's room. She was the advisor for the school paper, and it was time to finish the layout for the upcoming edition.

I was still upset about the talk with my parents and told Mrs. Conger about their resistance to me going to college and how frustrated I was with them.

"How can they be so stupid?" I said.

"Your parents are two of the best people I have ever met," she said, "and far from stupid."

I was embarrassed, sorry I had mentioned it to her, and went back to choosing font sizes for the headlines. She went back to grading tests.

Only years later did I learn from Mrs. Conger, who by then I was calling Doris, that she had gone to talk to my parents one day while I was at work, to try to help them understand why it was important to me to go to college. I'm glad I didn't know about it then. I would have worried about what embarrassing things they might have said to her.

One evening, the week after I sat down to talk my parents, Mother said, "Where's that application you need signed?"

I brought it downstairs, and she signed it.

"There you go," she said, and pushed it across the table to me.

"Thanks," I said, and that was the end of it.

That fall I went to college, and in subsequent years Sanford and Nancy went to college right out of high school, without any discussion or resistance, as far as I know. Just when I was so sure nothing would ever change, there was a new way of doing things.

# Leaving Home

When I was eighteen, I left home and never looked back. At least that's what I thought then. It felt less an escape than a wandering away while no one was paying attention.

I drove Dale's Corvair, white with red interior. He'd bought it with his own money. In a few days he'd be leaving for college too. He had waited a couple of years like he was supposed to, but as a freshman he couldn't have a car on campus. To save money, I'd be living with Abe and his family, and I needed a car to make the commute. Sure, I might miss out on some things by not living on campus, but I didn't care. I was going to college.

I'd been sorting through my belongings, deciding on the things I wanted to take with me, the things I wanted to leave behind. Some of the things I'd leave were obvious: clothes that embarrassed me with their differentness—handmade dresses and ill-fitting hand-me-downs, the aprons Mother said would protect those dresses so they'd last longer, as if that was a good thing.

I did not choose to take along my green shorts, an unsuccessful ninth-grade home economics project. The teacher gave us a choice, to make shorts or an apron. I chose shorts and found a piece of fabric in Mother's fabric drawer. It was an unattractive green, somewhere between mint and moss. Mother said there was no need to buy a new zipper. I tore one out of a brother's worn-out pants in the rag bag. The zipper was longer than the pattern called for, and I tried to adapt the pattern, but the zipper never worked. I had to wear those shorts for PE anyway. They were the only shorts I had, and they would have to do.

Our high school colors were red and white, and the PE uniforms they sold at the school store were red shorts and a white shirt that buttoned down the front. Mother said I could buy the shirt, but the official shorts were too short, too red, and, anyway, I had the green shorts, which went almost to my knees. I fastened them down the side with three safety pins. When we played field hockey or soccer, I wore the shirttail of my gym shirt out, and the safety pins on the green shorts were mostly hidden. But gymnastics was different. I hated the gymnastics unit, especially tumbling. If my shirttail went up, I knew anyone could see the safety pins on my homemade shorts, the shorts I was happy to leave behind in the bottom dresser drawer when I left for college, along with the aprons and the cape dress Mother had made for my baptism.

I carefully folded the clothes I wanted to take, most of them things I had bought with my own money, and packed them in the blue American Tourister suitcase Abe had bought me as a graduation gift. Later, when I had access to television, I saw it on a commercial being dropped from an airplane and landing undamaged, contents intact.

I included my navy blue cardigan, the one I'd worn with the gold circle pin for my yearbook picture, and the gray A-line skirt I'd bought already made. I did not need to roll it up at the waistband to make it shorter. I packed the jumpers Grace had made for me and hemmed to my specifications, still modest, but not embarrassingly long.

On my desk I had stacked the books I wanted to take, including my twelfth-grade literature textbook, *England in Literature*. We were supposed to turn in textbooks at the end of the year, but I had filled the margins with notes, trying to write down all the important things Mrs. Conger had said. I couldn't possibly erase them all. I offered to pay for the book, but Mrs. Conger said I should keep it. I had written so many notes on the *Rubaiyat of Omar Khayyam*, I could scarcely read the excerpt. In the margin I had written, "carpe diem—if you take care of the present, the past and future will take care of themselves."

I had underlined sections throughout the textbook. In the front I'd put index cards with quotes I wanted to keep. I had already memorized most of them but wrote them out in case I wanted to put them on a bulletin board over my desk.

"They also serve who only stand and wait." (Milton)

"And much it grieved my heart to think what man has made of man." (Wordsworth)

"Beauty is truth, truth beauty—that is all ye know on earth and all ye need to know." (Keats)

"Glory be to God for dappled things." (Hopkins)

I had circled metaphors and similes and remembered how excited I had been the first time I understood how they worked, the dazzling realization that anything, a word or object or event, could be much more than what it was. I wanted to find the layers of meaning buried out of sight. I couldn't imagine how it would be to create a metaphor of my own.

I wished I had kept the textbook from eleventh grade, *The United States in Literature*, but I had carefully erased my notes and turned it in. I hadn't had the courage to ask if I could keep it. I memorized poems from that textbook too, copying them and taping them to the pipes in front of the tub where Nancy and I washed eggs. I memorized "Hope Is the Thing with Feathers," "Stopping by Woods on a Snowy Evening," "Mending Wall," and "The Road Not Taken." On another index card I'd written the final lines of Frost's poem: "Two roads diverged in the woods, and I— I took the one less traveled by, and that has made all the difference."

In the stack to take along were my dictionary and my Bible. Of course I took my Bible. How could I have left it behind? It had taken on new appeal for me after I discovered it was crammed with metaphors. "I am the light of the world"; "Ye are the salt of the earth"; "The Lord is my shepherd." All those posters on the walls at Crystal Flow Camp! Now I knew that most of them were metaphors. Back then I thought they were simply Bible verses. The realization that some of what was written in the Bible could be metaphorical put it in a whole new light for me.

I flipped through my high school yearbook before putting it in the box. The notes from friends covered the photographs and went into the white margins. Suzanne remembered all the talks we'd had, especially about "that certain boy," and Judy and Marilyn mentioned those fun yearbook meetings. My English teacher, the one I'd written about on my college essay as "The Person I Admired," wrote almost a full page next to her picture. At the end of her note she'd written, "Best of everything to my 'solitary reaper.' Please let me know the ebb and flow of your tide." I loved her note, read it over and over, thrilled to be seen as having perhaps set myself apart as a student. It was an extraordinary feeling to be a Wordsworthian metaphor. I had never before felt so special.

I packed the Wiss scissors Charles had given me for high school graduation. It was an odd gift, but useful. Those scissors would never cut the pieces for homemade clothes, but there was so much else they would do. I'd use them to cut woolen skirts into strips to make braided rugs, make patches for quilts, or cut holiday wrapping paper. I packed my checkbook from Gap National Bank, where I'd been saving money in my own account for years. By lunch time I had my belongings organized and packed into boxes. I was ready to load the car.

At the table for lunch we bowed our heads for silent grace. I heard a fly buzz on the fly strip suspended from the fluorescent light over the table. Daddy cleared his throat to signal "Amen" and put the water pitcher on the floor beside his chair. Mother, who'd spent most of the morning cleaning in the milk house, filled our bowls with vegetable soup. She began passing around the plate of bread, and another of bologna and tomatoes to make sandwiches. I sat next to her and could smell the detergent she'd used to clean the milking machines. The lunch conversation was mostly about bacteria. No one mentioned I was moving out.

"I've done what I can," Mother said, "soaked all the milker hoses in the disinfectant and ran the brush through every space I could fit it in."

"Well, we're going to be in a fix if those numbers are still up when the milk inspector comes back," Daddy said.

"It all looked clean to me. I couldn't see a thing."

"You know bacteria's nothing you can see," Daddy said, slathering mayonnaise on his bread.

"Sucked water through the hoses, hot as I could get it," Mother said.

Washing the milking machines was mostly women's work, like washing dishes. I'd done it lots of times, but, if the milk inspector found a
problem, Mother was in charge.

There were six of us around the table for lunch. When Dale and I
were gone, it would be Sanford and Nancy and my parents, just those
four. Mother dished more soup. I crumbled saltines into mine. After
lunch I helped clean off the table and washed the dishes.

Mother may have glanced at me loading the car as she walked toward
the field to pick lima beans. She carried an empty bucket and wore her
sunbonnet and unlaced dusty black garden shoes. She had on an apron
over her faded cotton dress. She did not acknowledge that I, the tenth
of her twelve children, was leaving that day, whether or not anyone was
paying attention.

Even if she didn't say anything, Mother must have given my leaving
some thought. Surely she would have included me in her prayers the
night before as she knelt by the bed. I don't know what she might have
prayed. That I not leave home? That I return? Somehow I don't think
so. Although I will never know, I sometimes felt that Mother saw in
me, her strong-willed daughter, her own young self. Maybe I was pursuing the sort of future she dreamed of before she became a farmer's
wife and mother to all those children. This may not have been true at
all, but believing it made it easier for me to leave.

Her silent prayers were her own, and I don't know what she prayed
that night nor for all those other hundreds, maybe thousands, of hours,
kneeling by her bed. She may have implored God to give her daughter the strength to resist Satan's temptations as she went out into the
world. If she did, I didn't mind at all. How could it hurt, having an extra
shield against evil. I wasn't sure what to make of Satan. The preachers
said he walked the earth to create evil and rejoiced in stoking the eternal
fires of hell. As much as I doubted and questioned, I could not totally
let go of a nagging fear about the power of Satan.

A few days before I left home I had written on a piece of paper "I will
work to get the best grades I can and stay on the Dean's List. I will not

spend my time at college looking for a husband." I folded the piece of paper and put it under a stack of letters I would take along. I was determined to prove my father wrong about the worth of my going to college. I doubt either of those things I wrote down was in Mother's prayer. They weren't in my prayers. They were merely promises I made to myself, and writing them down seemed to make them more official.

It was strange that I should mention not looking for a husband. Throughout high school I had not dated, not even thought much about it. Although Mennonite boys often dated non-Mennonite girls, the reverse seldom happened, and I had not met any boys at church I had the least interest in. Although I was friends with lots of non-Mennonite boys in high school, dating them would never have been a consideration, from their side or mine. I did not spend much time thinking about being a wife or a mother, but it seemed inevitable. I assumed I would one day find a husband—it seemed like what young women were expected to do, and what older siblings had done—but I was not then dreaming of a house with a white picket fence, only of a world without fences.

In the weeks before I left home, each morning the weather had gotten a little cooler, and it wouldn't be long before the first frost. Maybe Mother was thinking about that as she went out to pick lima beans. At the first hint of frost, she picked everything still growing in the field and garden to make end-of-garden relish. The cabbage still needed to be harvested, chopped, and put into five-gallon crocks with salty brine to ferment for sauerkraut. I wouldn't be around to help with the cabbage or to pick up my share of the potatoes.

It didn't take me long to load my belongings into the car, putting the blue suitcase in the small trunk in the front and the few boxes in the back seat. I was ready to go, but no one dropped what they were doing and ran out to the car to hug me goodbye or wish me well. There were no photos to record the day, no good luck charms for me to take along. I could have been the one to initiate the hugging, tracking down my parents wherever they were working, and saying goodbye, or my brothers and sister. But it never occurred to me. That was not how we showed our love, not then anyway.

I don't remember when we became a family of huggers. I could not then have imagined there would ever be a time that every family gathering began and ended with everyone hugging everyone, sometimes twice if they lost their way in the group and couldn't remember who they had already hugged.

The Corvair purred as I turned the key in the ignition. I drove by the stripping room, which hadn't been used for stripping tobacco in my memory, but yet we called it the stripping room. I drove by the oddly named forebay, where the dog lay sleeping next to the tractor. I went past the milk house, where, in some dark corner, despite all of Mother's efforts, bacteria might still be lurking.

I drove by the asparagus patch, the feathery plants long since gone to seed, and the raspberries. Brambles, they were called in a British novel I had read. It could have been Jane Austen. I thought brambles sounded more poetic, and that's what I called them . . . but only in my own mind.

I shifted into second gear as I drove beneath the canopy of catalpa trees, which had started to shed their long pods. Nancy and Sanford and I once made a game of collecting the long green pods into baskets. With so many real things to harvest, I don't know why we needed to play harvest, but we did it nonetheless.

At the end of the lane stood the mailboxes, ours and our neighbors. All those mornings I had watched for the mailman, waited for him to stuff the mail into the box, and I'd race down the lane to be the first one to get to the mail. The envelopes seldom had my name on them, but I loved the mail anyway. The family diaspora had been going on for years, and we received long newsy letters from Rhoda in Ithaca, from Milt on Long Island, Grace in New York City, Ray at Penn State, Charles in Philadelphia. I found my siblings' lives fascinating beyond imagining. I couldn't wait to read every word of their letters and hoped I might one day be writing such letters myself.

I turned right onto Denlinger Road. I wasn't sure which Denlinger family the road was named for, but I knew the road had not been named for our family. We probably hadn't even been considered. I shifted into fourth gear and did not glance at the road banks where I had picked violets and bluebells when I walked back from the bus stop in elementary school.

By the time I got to the bus stop, tasks on the farm were no doubt being redistributed to adjust for one less person to help. Nancy would need to clean and grade and crate the eggs alone—no one to help her or argue with her or sing with her down in the windowless basement room. Who would open the gate to the pasture and bring the cows in for milking? That day Mother might do it when she finished picking lima beans.

I turned left at the bus stop where for all those years I had waited with my brothers and sisters. On cold winter mornings the wait felt like it went on forever. I did not think about those years or my brothers and sisters. With the family at home dwindled to four, the kitchen table leaves would need to come out; otherwise, the four remaining family members wouldn't be able to reach to pass the food around. The table would look small in the big kitchen.

I drove past the chinchilla farm, now a used car lot. I had never heard of chinchillas before that farm was built on a piece of land purchased from a neighbor. We went to the open house when they invited the community, eager to see those animals we had never heard of. Ours was not a "fur coat" sort of town, so they were not growing the chinchillas for our coats. I did not glance at the chinchilla farm as I drove by. I did not care why it came or why it left. That day I was leaving.

On the edge of the fields across the highway from Uncle Clarence's farm, a series of signs read: "Every day we do our part to make your face a work of art. Burma Shave." It was probably a metaphor, but for all the times I'd driven by, I'd never given it much thought, and I didn't on that day either.

I drove away, leaving behind the fields that only years later, when I revisited them, would evoke a calming and comforting nostalgia. That day I scarcely noticed them.

# PART THREE

# Making It to the Main Line

Four years of college passed in a blur of blue books and babysitting, with hundreds of hours on the road as I commuted from my brother Abe's house to college. When Dale took his white Corvair back at the end of my first year, I made the drive in the Bahama Blue VW Beetle Abe helped me purchase.

To get the most from my investment in education, I scheduled as many English courses as I could while also taking enough German literature for a double major. I signed up for the education courses that I would need for a teaching certificate. My financial aid package required me to keep up with a variety of tedious work-study jobs. Somehow I fit it all in.

Back at Abe's house, when I wasn't studying, I spent hours in the carefree world of four young children whose lives were very different from what my childhood had been. Playing on the floor, we built exciting block structures, put together puzzles, and rode the sturdy wooden train around the family room. We watched *Romper Room* and *Captain Kangaroo*, shows I had never seen. I pretended Miss Marcia could actually see us through her magic mirror, and Mr. Green Jeans knew something about farming. In summer I took the kids to the swimming pool almost every day. I loved reading Dr. Seuss books to them. There were no martyrs, no miracles, just happy, rhythmic language. I didn't for a moment consider whether the books were edifying. The kids seemed to consider me part child, part responsible adult, and I needed experience with both. It was unusual, but delightful, that four of my closest associates during my college years were children under six.

Living so far from campus and with other responsibilities, I had little time for a typical college life. Sometimes I envied my friends their dormitory experiences, with unlimited time to hang out with other students and pursue whatever distractions they chose; at other times I was happy to have a room and study of my own to return to at the end of the day. Nothing felt more important than learning all I could and doing well. I didn't allow for the possibility of not making the dean's list. Doing well was the thing I was sure I could succeed at, so I focused on that. I could organize and memorize, write papers, and present ideas. As long as I had that, I was certain all the rest would fall into place.

I sometimes joined friends at college football games. It was a sport I knew nothing about, all that crashing into each other, measuring, and lining up again and again. We'd had only soccer as a fall sport at our high school, so I had never seen football played anywhere. I found the sport confusing and illogical, but I went along anyway and cheered enthusiastically for the Flying Dutchmen of Lebanon Valley College.

Over the summer after my first year I briefly dated a guy who was working with a landscaping company doing work at Abe's office. He was on summer break from college. I had never really dated, so, when he asked me out, I thought it was time and said yes. Although we didn't have much in common, he seemed nice enough. We had gone out several times, when one evening, after his awkward groping had gotten him nowhere, he said, "You've got to come along to my grandmother's birthday party next week. She'd love you." I don't remember how it went beyond that. He wasn't a bad guy, so I hope I let him down gently, but we did not go out again. I never met his grandmother, so I don't know how she would have responded to me. It did not seem like we had enough to build a relationship around.

There were a few more half-hearted attempts at dating during my college years, efforts so unremarkable I remember little about them.

After the first year of college, I spent a good deal of time in an off-grounds house where a group of women students lived. Some of them were my friends, especially Gretchen, another English major. One day, as we were studying together for a Shakespeare test, she said, "You know, if you keep hanging out here, people are going to assume you're a lesbian." I laughed. How could she even suggest something so outrageous? I knew what a lesbian was. I had read about Gertrude Stein and Alice B. Toklas, but it certainly did not have anything to do with me. They were a fun group, the women who lived in that house, and I continued being Gretchen's friend without much concern that someone might think I was a lesbian. The idea was so preposterous, I barely gave it a thought.

At that time I would have said there were no gay men or lesbians in my world, but I know now that there were relatives, teachers, neighbors. I was naive enough to assume they were roommates or friends or happily single.

One of my best college friends was a German exchange student. I helped her with her English courses, and she helped me with German. She lived off-campus with a family, which made my experience feel less abnormal. We could be on the outside of the college experience together. She had learned much of her American English by watching Elvis Presley movies and Westerns, neither of which I had ever seen. Instead of saying "Goodbye," she sometimes said, "Keep your powder dry," as if that's what everyone in the United States said. She was happy to have an American friend and treated me as if I were a typical college student. I'm sure she recognized I wasn't, but it didn't matter. We shared hours of laughter, and hers is one of the few college friendships I maintained into adulthood.

I was in the last semester of college when, at the end of a student teaching seminar one afternoon, Dr. Herr, who directed the student teacher program, announced, "Next week recruiters from the Tredyffrin-Easttown School District will be here interviewing for teaching positions. The suburban Philadelphia schools are some of the best in the state, and they pay well. Let me know if you'd like to set up a time."

Without thinking much about it, I signed up for an interview slot. Why not? I needed a job, and I'd done well with my student teaching.

My mentoring teacher said I was one of the best student teachers she'd seen. She was only in her late twenties or early thirties, but still she'd seen more than a few student teachers. And I thought I deserved a job teaching at a good school.

I filled out an application and signed a release for my transcript. I arrived a few minutes early for the interview in the conference room at the education office, not sure what to expect. When I was called in, I sat down opposite the recruiter at the table. The interview was brief.

"What do you think are the most important considerations with teaching?" he asked.

"For me the most important thing is to encourage students to think and to love learning, not just memorize facts for the test," I said, not at all sure that's what he was going for with such a general question. I hoped he didn't ask a follow-up question, perhaps asking for examples.

If he asked, I didn't know what I might say. I'd had students memorize passages from Shakespeare and deliver them in front of the class. Did that kind of memorization teach a love of learning? Did it encourage them to think?

"Anything else you consider important?" he continued.

"I think a teacher needs to get to know the students and realize they are all unique and may be interested in different things and learn in different ways."

If he'd asked about my philosophy of teaching, I don't know what I would have said. At twenty-one, with one semester's teaching experience, I'm not sure I had thought about a philosophy. If I'd had my wits about me, I might have said, "Socratic," and it might have been true, if a bit pretentious. For student teaching, I was always prepared with notes, but I most enjoyed the class discussions that were more of a conversation with the students. At the end of the interview, I said I'd prefer to teach senior high, since that's where my experience had been.

"Do you think that would be a problem, since you'd be so close in age?"

"Not at all," I said.

The recruiter took notes, excused me, and went on to the next applicant.

A few weeks later I was called to the high school for an interview with Mr. Zettelmoyer, the principal. He was impressed with my transcript and letters of reference; he said I seemed like a "young lady with a good head on her shoulders" and offered me a job teaching senior high English. It had all been so easy. My first interview, and I had a teaching job. That school district paid a higher salary than most for beginning teachers, so I was sure I'd be able to start paying off my loans. Things were all falling into place.

Driving back to Abe's house after the interview, I stopped by the farm to see my parents.

"I got a job teaching outside Philadelphia," I said. "It's a great school, and they pay their teachers well."

"Glad you could get something," Daddy said, "all those loans to pay off."

"Well, that's what you wanted. To be a teacher," Mother said, sliding the roast into the oven.

I'm sure I wanted them to say more, maybe that college had been worth it for me, or that going directly out of high school had made sense. It would have been good to hear they were proud I had done well. I should have known better than to expect it, but it would have been nice.

I didn't know much about suburban Philadelphia before moving there. I did not even know it was called the Main Line, a string of towns stretched out along the railroad line and Route 30, the road that, if you stayed on it for fifty miles, passed within sight of our farm. At home we had called it the Lincoln Highway. The people who lived in suburban Philadelphia called the road Lancaster Avenue. The limit of my experience with the area was driving through it with my family on our way to the Philadelphia Zoo for rare summer outings. And Abe had lived in the area while he did his medical residency.

Lancaster Avenue was, no doubt, a route familiar to my Hostetter ancestors. Two hundred and fifty years earlier, Jacob and Anna, two of the first Hostetter immigrants, arrived in colonial Philadelphia. They were two of the many persecuted refugees William Penn had offered land leases and religious freedom when they were uprooted from their European homes. On their way to Lancaster County, Jacob and Anna must have taken the route that was now the main road. Back then it might have been a muddy path. Most of their descendants stayed in Lancaster County for eight generations, each settling no more than a few miles from their parents. Now I, part of the ninth generation, was driving in the other direction. I did not then think about those first Hostetters, or consider what I was fleeing from. Or going to.

It was 1968 when I began teaching. Some journalists called it "The Year That Changed History." Robert Kennedy and Martin Luther King Jr. were assassinated within months of each other. The war in Vietnam had gotten so unpopular that thousands were marching in protest. The year before, *Time* magazine chose as their "Person of the Year" people aged twenty-five and under. I was one of them. I was aware of what was going on, shocked by the assassinations and upset about the war, but I was not actively involved. For me, going to an anti-war rally in Washington, DC, or to Woodstock the following year would have been as unlikely as undertaking a vision quest to the Australian outback. I had responsibilities, loans to repay. I needed to prove that I was deserving of my education. I had no space for that sort of rebellion or the freedom of rootlessness.

I rented a room in an elderly woman's home within walking distance of the high school. It was inexpensive, and her family was happy to have me living there in case something happened to her. She assigned me a shelf in the cupboard and a section in the refrigerator where I could keep my food.

I was nervous on my first day of teaching but felt confident as I stood in front of the eleventh-grade English class. It was one of the advanced classes, and Mr. Zettelmoyer had told me that all the students in those classes went to college. They knew they needed to do well. They sat at their desks with their notebooks open and pens poised, waiting to be taught, and I was their teacher. Although I was only a few years older than they were, I had no doubt I could do it. I told the students, "By this time I am assuming all of you know your grammar, so our focus this year will be on literature and writing and, most importantly, thinking. I'm going to expect a lot of you."

I expected a lot of myself too, and teaching was not easy. Preparations for five classes, plus grading tests and papers, took a lot of time. Some more experienced teachers, taking a cigarette break in the teachers' lounge, said it didn't need to be as hard as I made it. One of the guys in the social studies office, where I sometimes went to hang out at lunchtime, said, "Assigning essay questions is just asking for extra work. What ever happened to spelling tests?"

I wanted my students to love learning as much as I had and not just love doing well. I had told them I would teach them to think. Although I wasn't sure where to begin to reach for such a lofty goal, I was certain spelling tests were not the right approach. I wanted to be the teacher some of my teachers had been to me, the kind of teacher who made you believe in yourself and realize how exciting learning was. I realized my education classes in college had not taught me those things, but I was sure I could somehow pass them on to my students.

# Among the Right People

One of my first friends at the school was Charlotte, who had been teaching for many years, and it was she who told me about *The Right People*, a book by Stephen Birmingham. She lent it to me, and I read it, including the chapter about the Main Line, one of the "right" places for "The Right People" to live, along with Grosse Pointe, Michigan; Westchester County, New York; Hartford, Connecticut . . . places I knew nothing about. The book was about people who had made it in the social establishment, and here I was, apparently living among them. Charlotte seemed to care about old and new money, one of the central themes of *The Right People*. Her family appeared to have money, but I didn't know if it was old or new. Coming from no money, as I did, the distinction seemed odd.

As nearly as I could tell, the thing that was important about money was whether you were born with it and how your family had earned it. I knew without doing any research that "old money" did not come from selling eggs and fresh vegetables on a market route in Coatesville. Certainly not from trapping mice and filling jelly jars with potato bugs to earn money from my parents.

Yet I was curious about *The Right People* and another book, *The Social Registry*, that Birmingham mentioned. I had never heard of it and had no idea where you would find such a book, but the people listed in it probably knew exactly where to find it. Being listed in the book was proof you were one of them.

When I drove down Montgomery Avenue, past an impressive gated entrance to a sprawling estate with stables, tennis court, and swimming pool, I wondered if some of the Right People might live there. The book mentioned places they were known to gather, places I'd never have occasion to go, like the Merion Cricket Club or the Radnor Hunt Club. From what I read, horses were as important to the Right People as old money, and the annual Devon Horse Show was an event mentioned in the book. I drove by the horse show grounds frequently. It was on Lancaster Avenue, just a couple of miles from where I lived.

"Devon Horse Show just opened," Charlotte said one day as we walked out of school together. "Want to go one afternoon?"

"Can anyone go?"

"Of course," she said, "You can buy general admission tickets. We won't be sitting in a reserved box, but we'll be able to see everything from the stands."

"Why not," I said. "I don't know anything about horse shows. It'll be fun." We made plans to go the next afternoon.

After Charlotte and I paid our admission and went inside the gate, I was surprised to see all the booths, tidy stables, food stands, and white fences. It was like a little village in the horse show grounds. Some of the people milling about were dressed up; others looked like they had come directly from the garden or stable. Many of them seemed to know each other. I didn't recognize anyone. We found a seat in the stands, not far from the boxes.

"You think those are some of the Right People?" I said, glancing toward the reserved boxes where many of the women wore brightly printed dresses and colorful hats.

"Could be," Charlotte said, "but they're not always who you think they are."

Whoever they were, I knew I was not one of them and never would be. They were most certainly not renting rooms from old ladies in dusty dark houses and keeping their food on assigned shelves.

Charlotte and I watched as beautiful horses and elegant riders sailed gracefully over the jumps. Horses had been common in the landscape of my childhood, pulling Amish buggies on back roads or farm equipment in neighboring fields, but the horses jumping at the Devon Horse Show seemed like totally different animals. I could not imagine the horses I had seen pulling buggies or farm implements sailing over the jumps at the horse show.

The first years of being on my own were busy. In addition to the work involved with teaching, I wanted to catch up on the experiences I had missed in my earlier years. I wanted to be a woman who went places, who did things. If Charlotte suggested driving down to Ocean City, New Jersey, after school one day to have dinner at her favorite seafood restaurant, I'd do it. If a friend thought taking the train to New York City for a museum day might be fun, I happily went along. I went to concerts—Bob Dylan, Joan Baez, Arlo Guthrie, Simon and Garfunkel. I went to hear the Philadelphia Orchestra, saw performances by the Alvin Ailey Dance Company, and went to movies whenever I felt like going, without a thought about whether they were edifying. It was finally my chance, and I couldn't get enough of the things I had not been able to do growing up. I never considered if it violated Mennonite rules. I was on my own and could do whatever I chose.

When the lights went down in the theater the first time I saw Judith Jamison and the Alvin Ailey Dancers, I didn't know what to expect. I didn't know much about any kind of dance, since it was one of the amusements church teachings had forbidden. I had by that time seen ballet, but this was different. When Judith Jamison appeared on stage, it was like she became water or air. When the company danced *Revelations*, I wept. There was something about the glorious spirituals they danced to, the flowing white dresses, the gorgeous bodies, the way they moved. I was transfixed as they danced to "Wade in the Water," and I was speechless as we left the theater.

"How did you like it?" my friend asked as we walked to the car.

"It was like poetry in motion," I said, knowing it was a trite thing to say and didn't begin to explain how the performance had moved me.

It didn't take me long to break many of the rules of my upbringing. I wore slacks, shorts, and miniskirts. I had my ears pierced. I missed

Sunday worship services more than occasionally. From time to time on a Friday, I found myself at Connus Alehouse Happy Hour with my teaching colleagues.

The staff I taught with frequently got together for parties or cookouts. Since I was single, I often went on my own, sometimes with friends. At a staff holiday party, I found myself cornered by a man I worked with. Before I really understood what was happening, he was pressing himself against me, kissing me, pushing his tongue into my mouth. I finally got away and avoided him for the rest of the evening. He acted as if he thought he was doing me a favor with his intrusive pawing, and I should be flattered by the attention. Although I found his behavior disgusting, it would not then have occurred to me to report him to a superior. He was, after all, a department head. The only thing I could think to do was stay away from him if I saw him at school or at subsequent events.

It would not be the last time being a woman alone made me vulnerable. When I finally saved up enough money to afford an apartment of my own, I was thrilled that I would no longer need to negotiate with housemates about dishes left in the sink, dirty showers, spoiled food, or any of the other issues of shared living that had caused me conflicts. My apartment was on the third floor of a rambling Victorian house that had been turned into five units.

One afternoon a man who had just moved in across the street saw me struggling to get my bike chain back on and came over to help. We spoke to each other a few times over the next week, and one evening he showed up at my door. I thought nothing of letting him in. He seemed like a nice guy, and he was my neighbor. Within minutes, he was all over me, kissing and groping. Only after repeated requests did he stop, angry and frustrated with me that I would not cooperate. He stormed out. A week later, he showed up again, demanding that I let him in. When I threatened to call the police, he finally left. After that I was much more careful about who I spoke to, much more hesitant about opening the door. I resented feeling vulnerable. Living on my own did not seem like it should be an invitation for men to prey on me.

Horseback riding lessons were Bonnie's idea. She was also an English teacher, and she became a close friend.

"I've always wanted to take horseback riding lessons, haven't you," she said at a Friday afternoon Happy Hour.

I hadn't really, but it seemed something every well-raised young woman on the Main Line should do . . . yet another thing for me to catch up on. So I said, "Sure."

Bonnie and I signed up for a beginning class at Paoli Stables. It was spring, and I liked the idea of being outdoors for a couple hours one afternoon a week. On my first day of riding class, I was assigned a horse named Star. We made it through walking that first week, and, in subsequent weeks, posting, trotting, and cantering. The young instructor frequently corrected my form. I pretended I understood what she meant when she told me to change my diagonals, but I really didn't.

Bonnie dropped out first, and I was left on my own to start low jumping. I had seen the famous Rodney Jenkins at the Devon Horse Show when he and his beautiful horse had soared over jumps. I was amazed a horse so big could defy gravity and that Rodney could stay on his back with such apparently effortless poise. I knew it could be done.

As Star and I approached the first jump, a jump so low Star could have stepped over it, I felt my saddle slip sideways. It was a slow-motion movement I didn't know how to stop. I pulled my boots out of the stirrups and dropped gently to the dirt. Star stepped over the jump and continued around the ring, saddle askew.

The young riding instructor walked over from the center of the ring to make sure I was all right. I stood up and dusted off my jeans. The dirt brushed off easily, not like real dirt at all. I was used to farm dirt. I'm not sure anything could have grown in the dirt in the riding ring. I caught up with Star, who did not protest as I led him back to the stable and took off his saddle. I brushed him down and told the teacher I was finished for the day. I never returned to Paoli Stables and have never again seen the need to get back on a horse.

During my first year of teaching, my parents moved off the farm and into a smaller house in town. With their children gone, my parents, then in their mid-sixties, could not keep up with the farm work on their own. All of us had moved on to lives away from the farm and community of our upbringing, and none of us was interested in taking over the farm. My brothers who were farmers had already purchased their own farms. For my parents, adjustment to life off the farm was challenging. I felt like I had moved a very long way from home, but, in fact, I was only an hour's drive away and made it home frequently. When I visited, I took out my earrings, took off my rings, wore a skirt rather than slacks or shorts. Part of me still wanted to be a good girl by my parents' definition. I don't know what I thought might happen if I wore jewelry or slacks or mentioned doing something they might disapprove of. A fear of hellfire and an angry God had given way to a fear of disappointing my parents. After all, they had done their best, and I did not want them to feel that they had failed.

My parents may have had moments of wondering where they had gone wrong since many of their children had wandered in ways most of their friends' and relatives' children had not. It was not for their lack of teaching or insistence on regular church attendance. They had done their part. As many of my siblings left the Mennonite Church and became Presbyterians or Methodists or Quakers, or nothing at all, it may well have given my parents pause. I remembered Mother's anguish the day she learned that one of my older brothers had joined the Presbyterian Church.

By the time Neil Armstrong took his historic stroll on the moon, I had finished a year of teaching and had purchased my first television, a thirteen-inch black and white. Since my parents had no TV, I loaded mine into my VW and made the drive to their home so they could watch the moon landing.

I set up the TV in the corner of the living room and adjusted the whip antenna. Mother and I sat in rocking chairs next to each other and watched coverage until midnight. Daddy said it was past his bedtime and left us to wait for the moonwalk. We watched as the grainy figure wearing his otherworldly moon suit took his first bouncy steps and planted the flag.

"I'm not sure it's right," Mother said. "I'm not sure man was meant to go to the moon."

"It's historical," I said.

"Yes, but I'm sure it will affect the weather. The garden will probably never be the same."

She needn't have worried. For all the space exploration, my parents and their garden would thrive for another thirty years.

It felt strange being one-on-one with my parents when I went home to visit. With none of my siblings around, I got more individual attention than I was accustomed to. Sometimes more than I wanted.

On one visit, after Mother had served cake and snow pudding for dessert, Daddy said, "If you died, what would you want us to put in your obituary about your church affiliation?"

We hadn't been talking about church, although I knew it was never far from my parents' minds, and we hadn't been talking about obituaries either. I didn't read obituaries as regularly as they did, but I knew that in the Lancaster *Intelligencer Journal*, most obituaries included church membership.

Surprised at Daddy's question, I blurted out something like "I guess that won't be my problem." I'm sure I sounded more flip than I intended, but I doubt I was the only person in my mid-twenties who hadn't given much thought to wording for my obituary.

"Do you still consider yourself a Mennonite?" he continued.

"I don't know how it works," I said. "Do they let you know if you've been put out?"

"When's the last time you went to Communion?"

"It's been a while."

I knew it was important to attend Mennonite Communion twice a year, and I had kept up with that expectation during most of college, taking my prayer covering out of the drawer in the bottom of my jewelry box, where it was stored except for those times I needed to attend a Mennonite church. When I went for Communion, I would wait to put the covering on until I got to the church parking lot. Sometimes I went to my parents' church, sometimes another church that was part of the same Mennonite conference.

"Church membership is something you should give some thought to," Daddy said.

"I guess if they haven't let me know they put me out, you could put in my obituary that I'm a Mennonite," I said. "If it makes you feel better."

"That's an awful thing to say." Daddy's voice was quivering.

The topic of my obituary never came up again. If I went to church while I was living on the Main Line, I went to either a Quaker Meeting or a Unitarian service, where the sermons focused more on philosophy or poetry than scripture. I found the silence of the Quaker Meeting nurturing, and their belief in God as a force for good in all people felt right to me, much better than believing in an angry God watching to see how often I violated any of the arbitrary rules the male leaders of the Mennonite Church had set. I don't know if my parents would have considered either Quaker or Unitarian real religions, so, in my attempt to avoid conflict, I didn't mention attending those churches.

My parents' move from the farm, as necessary as it may have been, was disorienting. I wanted and needed to leave home, but I still wanted home to be there, solid and predictable, a world I could count on. It felt strangely unsettling to have my parents going through a dramatic change at the same time I was. It was hard for me to wrap my mind around them as townspeople, people whose schedules were not controlled by the rhythms of planting and harvest, the needs of cows and chickens. I tried to support them in their transition as I came to terms with my own.

# Where Do I Fit?

While I was living on the Main Line, even if I wasn't one of the "Right People," I worked hard to fit in, to come across as educated and sophisticated. For all those efforts, one of the main things I was known for was my connection to the quaint Mennonite culture of my upbringing. When the organizers of the adult evening classes were looking for someone to teach traditional quilting, they came to me for names, knowing I'd have connections in the Mennonite quilting community. An aunt and cousin came down from Lancaster County to teach the women of the Main Line to make traditional quilts. No matter how hard I tried, I couldn't shake my roots. It wasn't that I was any longer embarrassed about it, but I wanted to be known for more.

Among my new friends, I was the source of information on gardening, canning, pickling, or making apple butter. If friends had out-of-town visitors for the weekend, they would frequently ask me to go along for a day trip to Lancaster County. I was the perfect tour guide, showing them the back roads, away from buses filled with tourists. With my experience at Plain and Fancy, I was able to answer most of their questions. I often took them to our farm, where an Amish family now lived. We walked up the back path—the meadow hill, we had always called it—and looked at the view. From the top of the hill we could see the farm where Daddy had grown up, the farm my parents rented when they were first married, and, over a rise of land, the farm where Mother grew up. Our farm didn't feel the same at all. Outbuildings had been turned into horse stables, and horses were grazing in the orchard. All the electrical lines had been taken out. It felt familiar, yet different.

As much as I had wanted to get away, it was a strange feeling not having easy access to the farm, needing to ask permission to walk to the top of the hill and finding Amish children I didn't know wandering about. I was surprised how much I missed being able to go back whenever I wanted. I didn't feel like I belonged anymore, but I wanted to have the farm there, not so I could return and live in that world again but so I could brush against it now and then and remind myself of the parts of me I did not want to lose.

I became more and more comfortable with teaching and added new responsibilities and experiences. When they needed a faculty sponsor for the school newspaper, *The Spoke*, I signed up. In high school, I had been editor of the school paper, and Mrs. Conger, the teacher about whom I had written my college essay, was the sponsor. It seemed an obvious role for me.

Students at that time were in a rebellious frame of mind, convinced nothing was more important than challenging the norm. Members of the newspaper staff often stayed after school and hung out in the cluttered office adjacent to my classroom. They usually didn't have much to do but behaved as if it were a big-city newsroom, and they were waiting for fast-breaking news to come spilling out of a teletype machine.

Harry, the editor, looking at us through the mop of hair hanging over his eyes, said, "For the next issue, I think we should do the whole editorial page about making school attendance voluntary. We could do a survey and have students make comments."

"Yeah," said one of the assistant editors, "and we could have an editorial about getting rid of the school board. They're the ones with the power, and they are totally out of touch."

"I think mandatory school attendance is a state law," I said.

"Well, it shouldn't be," Harry said. "If teachers are doing their jobs, classes would be so good kids would want to come to school."

"I think you should be realistic about what can be changed," I said.

"You have to look at the big picture," Harry said. "Like with the war. What if everyone had said there's no way to stop a war."

"I think it's good to start small," I said.

"I disagree. I think you should always go big."

I saw his point. When I was newspaper editor, I might have said the same thing, but I was an adult now. I knew the principal was counting on me to keep the students under control with what went into the paper, but I didn't always feel good about it. The students were encouraged to express their opinions . . . but only up to a point. I was expected to remind them of the limits.

Even though the high school administrators may not have been making the dramatic changes Harry and his newspaper staff might have wanted, they were making changes that reflected the experimental spirit of education at the time. A few years after I started teaching, the administrators decided that all English courses for juniors and seniors should be electives. One of the first courses I proposed was "Literature of War and Peace." I had taken an adult evening class in "Writings of Nonviolence" and was inspired by the works of Gandhi and Martin Luther King Jr. I had come a long way from my embarrassment in Mrs. Groff's sixth-grade class and, as a young teacher, would have proudly volunteered that my father, as well as my male relatives, were conscientious objectors and had not fought in any war. I was convinced of the value of pacifism and civil disobedience.

I added electives in "Literature of Adolescence and Aging" and "Literature of Future." Coming up with separate reading lists and lesson plans complicated preparation, but my classes were consistently filled and course evaluations positive. Sometimes I thought my goal of teaching students to think, or at least expecting them to, had not been too ambitious.

I spent hours in the evening poring over earnest eleventh-grade essays on topics such as whether Henry Fleming in *The Red Badge of Courage* was a hero or a coward, whether *Brave New World* or *1984* presented a more plausible projection of the future. I tried to evaluate how clear the topic sentences were, how thoughtful and convincing the arguments, and how many punctuation errors were too many to earn an A. Sometimes, after sleeping on it, I'd come back to an essay and add a plus, or a minus, to the grade, as if a career depended on it, theirs *or* mine. I wanted to be sure of myself. Parents at the high school where I taught were involved in their children's education, and I was always aware I might need to defend a grade.

Not everything teaching-related was serious work. Every spring the teachers in the school district presented a musical to raise money for a scholarship fund. One of my friends was in charge of choreography for *Anything Goes*, the musical chosen for the production. She asked if I would dance in the chorus line, and I agreed. I had no personal experience with dance, any kind of dance. Yet I wanted to be a good sport and do my part. My friend said it would be fun. Rehearsals were an ordeal for me. No matter how hard I tried to focus, I had trouble grasping the dance steps. I felt self-conscious and clumsy and was sure I stood out in the chorus line.

Although I knew the choreographer was kidding, I was embarrassed when she stopped the music at one rehearsal and asked me, laughing, "What do you call that dance you're doing?"

As if I would have known what the possibilities were.

I couldn't resist an opportunity for more education, especially if it was free. I completed the forms the first day the school district circulated the announcement that it would reimburse teachers for evening and summer courses taken toward their master's degrees. I applied to nearby Villanova University. I started course work in the summertime, and many of the students in the graduate classes were nuns from teaching orders. I had never been around nuns, and they were much more fun than I had expected. Since it was a Catholic school, some of the professors started each class by reciting the "Hail Mary." Sometimes, without thinking, especially if I was sitting near the nuns, I would find myself murmuring along.

After several years of summer and evening classes, I finished my master's. I thought I might get a PhD, maybe teach college one day.

One by one, my siblings had been getting married, and I knew it would soon be my turn. Marriage and children felt like a family expectation. Rhoda already had seven children. Of my siblings older than I, only Charles was still single.

I visited Charles one weekend when he was in graduate school in Baltimore. Although he never told me directly, I realized during that visit he might be in love with another man. He felt different, even the music he played. Instead of his usual classical music, he was listening to James Taylor and Joni Mitchell. He told me about a new friend, and I could overhear hushed phone conversations. He wasn't himself. I was shocked and saddened by the possibility he might be gay. As I made the hour-long drive home after the visit, I was so upset and distracted I wasn't sure if I should even be driving. I was shaken and confused. I admired him for so much, and this did not fit my idealized image of him.

When I got home, I called my friend Charlotte and told her about my suspicions. She was reassuring and said, even if it was true, there was no cause for alarm. She said she loved gay men, and they were usually great guys, some of her favorite people. But still? My brother? Gay? How could that be? I did not want to confirm my fears, so I did not ask him about it.

Looking back on that weekend, I'm not sure what my despair was about. I had never given any of it much thought, so I did not know what being gay might mean for him. I was certainly not then thinking of its implications for me.

One evening while I was sitting in the living room of my apartment grading papers, the phone rang. It was a student's father.

"Would you be interested in going to London over spring break?" he asked.

"What do you mean?" I had never been on an airplane and did not have a passport. Of course, I hadn't thought of going to London for spring break.

"Vicki would like to do a tour and thinks she can get enough friends to go along, if they can get an adult to chaperone. She thought of you. You'd go for free."

"I'll think about it," I said. I had traveled very little but wanted to be a woman of the world, so the idea had some appeal.

Vicki, one of my eleventh-grade students, brought me a packet of information the next day. The tour sounded well organized, tightly structured, with little free time. The group would go to the theater for three evening productions. Surely the students would be tired by the end of the day. The tour included other students from area high schools and their adult chaperones. I said I'd do it and ordered my first passport. Vicki easily found nine friends who wanted to go and whose parents could pay for it. Why shouldn't I go to London for spring break? For free.

I loved visiting the places I had heard and read about—the Tower of London, Stratford-upon-Avon, Buckingham Palace, Westminster Abbey. Standing in Poets' Corner in Westminster Abbey, I was in awe looking at the busts and plaques memorializing the people buried there. The writers whose words I had spent all those years studying, whose writings appeared in my *England in Literature* textbook, were buried in that place. The students did not find it very interesting, but, as I stood reading the names, it felt to me like sacred space.

Somehow, I naively believed that for the high school students, the trip was all about theater, history, and culture, as it was for me. They were not always as tired as I thought they'd be at the end of a highly scheduled day, and I hadn't anticipated how attractive the teenage girls would find any male with a British accent. Parents from one of the other groups let me know they had seen a few of my girls leaving after hours with a couple of the hotel bellhops. Such behavior would never have occurred to me as a teenager. With so much to see and learn, nothing would have been further from my mind.

I met with the girls the next morning before we got on the bus.

"You know leaving the hotel after curfew is against the rules," I said.

"It's not like we did anything," one of them said. "We were just trying to get to know the guys and see more of London."

"This is your warning," I said. "It would be a shame if you had to go home early. I know your parents would be disappointed."

For the next couple nights, I sat in the lobby after my students had gone to their rooms, to make sure they didn't sneak out again. No one needed to be sent home early.

Now that I had a passport, I didn't want it to go to waste. I traveled to Switzerland and Germany with Nancy for a few weeks one summer. She had done a student exchange program in Switzerland for a year and wanted to visit her host family and share some of her favorite places with me. We visited the areas of Switzerland where we thought our ancestors had lived, and we stood on the bank of the Limmat River in Zurich where many of the persecuted Mennonites had been drowned. We hiked in the Alps, took a cruise on the Rhine River, and spent time with my German friend from college.

The following year, I traveled to Nicaragua with my ten-year-old nephew and a teacher friend to visit Charles, who was working on a Public Health Service project in Puerto Cabezas, a small town on the Caribbean coast. In the outdated, bullet-ridden plane we took to fly across the country, we shared space with crates of live chickens and boxes of fruits and vegetables.

We went with Charles in a rickety outboard motorboat to a remote and primitive village where he provided basic medical care. The villagers welcomed him eagerly and thought he could work miracles. I was fascinated by the small world the villagers inhabited. They looked contented as they ground grain on dimpled rocks and fished from dugout canoes, depending on one another in their isolated community. I had no idea there were still places like this in the world. I had been so focused on establishing myself in the larger world, I did not realize how much I could learn from smaller worlds.

During the years I was teaching, I made friends easily and was never lacking for things to do or people to do them with. Yet I was sometimes lonely. I assumed I would one day find the right man for me, even though I had little inclination to seek him out. I did not give much thought to the reality that, of all the many men I had met, I hadn't really been attracted to any of them. As far as I knew, I had two options—

marrying a man or remaining single, becoming what Mother called "an unclaimed blessing." At that time I saw no other possibilities. I had moments of thinking it might be time to come to terms with being an unclaimed blessing, which didn't seem so bad. I certainly could not have imagined a future in which marrying another woman was a possibility.

I was the fun friend you'd invite to an event when a single brother or cousin was visiting from out of town, and having an even number of guests at the wedding reception or dinner party was important. I was invited to parties with my brother Ray's classmates at the veterinary school, then almost all male. My social life was active, and I thought it was enough.

For a few years I spent a good deal of time with Ted, a man I'd met through mutual friends. He taught in a nearby school district. We attended movies, plays, and concerts together. We went on summer road trips, hiking, biking, camping. We shared tents, cabins, and hotel rooms. Sometimes, lying next to him, I wondered why being intimate never seemed to occur to either one of us. Most people who knew us assumed we were, and I was fine with that. Although we didn't really talk about it, it was clear that neither of us had much interest in having our relationship move in that direction. It was purely platonic, and we had a great time together—he was smart and fun, and we shared many interests. Being with him made me feel less vulnerable and distracted me from feeling the need to date. I was, from all appearances, going out with Ted. Something about it was so comfortable, the secure feeling of appearing to have a boyfriend. I did not need to give up my independence or worry about commitment. I had someone to do things with.

One of my close friends said to me one day, "Your relationship with Ted doesn't seem to be going anywhere."

"Yeah," I said, "but he's a really fun guy." I knew she was right, and I did not mind at all. Nor did I give any thought to what it might mean. Only in retrospect, after finding out years later that Ted was gay, do I wonder if the invitations to accompany him to staff holiday parties or weddings was to allay suspicions from his friends or coworkers that he might be gay. And, although I was not aware of it at the time, I may have been using him in the same way.

I was living in my own apartment and had been able to save money and pay off most of my college loans. Since my father had feared a college debt might make me less appealing for marriage, I should have been in good shape. My life was all I thought I had wanted: success in a career I found fun and fulfilling, friends, opportunity to travel, and the freedom to wear or do whatever I chose. With my life filled with rich experiences, I didn't understand why I had moments of discontent. I wasn't sure what needed to change. I thought I might be overcommitted and simply had too much to do. For all my efforts, I didn't always feel that I fit into my new world, and I wasn't sure if I wanted to. In some ways I felt as out of place on the Main Line as I had on the farm, maybe more so. It sometimes felt I still had a yearning, but I was not certain what I was yearning for. It was no longer as clear as joining Girl Scouts or taking tap dancing lessons. It was more elusive than that.

I was eligible for a year's leave from teaching and decided to apply for a sabbatical. It would give me a break and time to clarify my goals. I wasn't thinking of leaving teaching, not after I had worked so hard to get there. It would only be a break, or so I thought. Teacher friends had come back from their time off reenergized from doing something different for a year. I was excited to have that happen for me too. I could never have imagined the direction the break would take me.

# Zeit und Raum

I never intended to become a cheesemaker. Of all the futures I might have imagined for myself as a young adult, certainly none involved raw milk. It was an unlikely path that brought me, in my late twenties, to the place where I was considering a job that could include making cheese.

I had been certain of a few things when at eighteen I drove away from the farm: I was leaving, I was going to college, I would become a teacher, and I most definitely was not going to be a farmer's wife and get stuck in Lancaster County for the rest of my life.

I couldn't wait to leave behind the cows, the milk house, the stable, and the big refrigerated tank of unpasteurized milk with its agitator slowly turning to keep the cream from rising. In spring the milk sometimes tasted so strongly of onion grass that Sylvan Seal, our milk company, rejected it. Mother, not wanting to let it go to waste, made every milk-based pudding she could think of and all the ice cream we could eat. All of it tasted like onion. But all the puddings and ice cream weren't enough, and gallons of milk were poured down the ditches or fed to the neighbor's pigs. When I left, I was relieved my life would never again be affected by the whims of milk.

When I was considering taking a sabbatical, I heard, quite by chance, of a temporary assignment managing a town development project in Helvetia, a remote West Virginia town. Nothing about the development project sounded very complicated, and, although it drew on skills I wasn't

133

sure I had, I thought I could acquire them. In my twenties, I approached most tasks with a "how hard can it be?" attitude.

The job description was vague, and the income seemed iffy. The woman who had started the project five years before, buying and reno- vating some of the vacant buildings in that small town, had to leave when she became seriously ill. After she left, the buildings stood empty, and the new owner needed someone to help get things up and run- ning. I understood I would be involved in managing and maintaining rental properties, developing a craft collective, and managing a restau- rant and small cheesemaking operation. In my more cautious middle years, I would not have so enthusiastically embraced such an oppor- tunity. It was an uncharacteristically impulsive decision for me. In my letter requesting the leave, I indicated I was interested in learning about another culture and collecting an oral history.

I got the job, applied for the leave, sublet my apartment, and priori- tized what I should take along for such an adventure. I hoped I would have time for reading and writing, and a break from the demands of teaching. I didn't spend much time thinking about what the responsi- bilities of the new position might be—just the freedom it would give me. I would be provided with a place to live, and I would have time. The rest I could certainly work out, and besides, it was only for a year.

I set off for Helvetia. The turnpike and interstate leg of the trip from suburban Philadelphia went quickly. I had packed every available cor- ner of the yellow VW I called Buttercup—replacing my Bahama blue beetle—from floor to ceiling, even the passenger seat. I had scarcely enough space to shift gears. In Virginia, beyond Staunton, I hit the foot- hills of the Appalachians, with uphills and downhills and switchbacks and more gear shifting than I'd ever had the need to do. When I thought I might be coming to a straightaway and could finally shift into fourth, there'd be another hill, another curve.

The directions I got from my contact in Helvetia were to "go to the end of nowhere, turn left at Mill Creek, and go another twenty miles." The narrow, twisting road beyond Mill Creek made the road from Staunton seem like an interstate. At the base of the last hill, the road bent to the right and led into Helvetia, nestled in the valley. A hand-lettered sign on a weathered cabin said *"Zeit und Raum ist alles"* . . . Time and space is everything.

I drove the short distance to the cottage that was to be my temporary home. It felt good not to be in motion anymore after the dizzying drive. The brown-shingled cottage could have been moved from the Alps, and it reminded me of the trip I'd taken to Switzerland with my sister Nancy a few years before. The shutters and window boxes were painted a soft greenish blue. The space inside felt cozy and comfortable, with low ceilings and afternoon sun streaming through the windows. The unfamiliar furniture, mostly well-worn antiques, quickly felt familiar. I carried in the box of books that included, among other things, my dictionary, a thesaurus, a collection of Emily Dickinson poetry, my favorite Loren Eisley books, and some of the Foxfire Books. I set up the stereo and organized my record albums. I carried in my typewriter and set up a desk space on a sturdy table by the window in the living room overlooking the backyard.

The new owner of the properties, a woman who had grown up in the area and recently returned, invited me for dinner the first night. She lived around the corner. Before dinner, we walked around town, and she showed me the restaurant, the craft store, and the cheese house. The power had been turned off, and the buildings closed up for years. They were dark and smelled musty. Windows were dirty, the sills filled with dusty cobwebs and dead flies. It was hard to believe, but she said all the spaces had been quite pleasant when they were up and running before. The cleaning alone felt like a daunting task, but I could clean. I knew I could clean. We went back to her house for dinner, shared a bottle of wine. She told me her dreams of restoring the town and preserving its heritage. Since I hadn't yet had time to dream my own dreams, I started with hers. As it was getting dark, I walked back to my new home and continued unpacking before going to bed. I slept well.

Helvetia made Gap, the town where I'd grown up, seem like a big city. The population of Helvetia and the surrounding farms totaled less than a hundred, and of those hundred, at least half were more than seventy-five years old. In many ways living in that cottage in Helvetia made no sense at all, and yet it felt like absolutely the right thing for me to be doing.

Many of my friends and family visited during those first few months. At the time I assumed they came because my calls and letters made the town sound so interesting and exotic, and that may have been a part of it, but I have since learned that they also came to check on me. They knew I had worked hard to put myself through college to become a teacher, and, from all reports, I had enjoyed teaching and done it well. Moving to a place so remote did not seem to fit. What was that about?

I can imagine how the conversations may have gone among siblings, aunts and uncles, parents, and friends during that time when many of them came to visit me:

"How did you think she was?"

"Well, she seemed happy enough, happy as I've ever seen her, but it's primitive, the way she lives. The well was low when we were there, and we had to carry buckets of water from the river to flush the toilet. We brought water from the spring for drinking."

"I thought she liked teaching. They didn't let her go, did they?"

"She does like teaching. It's a leave. She's going back in a year."

"Did she tell you she was writing a book this winter?"

"Just one? Should have time to write a couple. Not much else going on, if you ask me."

"Funny. She's seems right at home."

"It's a sweet little town. Scenic. But it's more like a museum or a movie set than a real town."

"And run a cheese factory? All she went through to put herself through college and get her master's, and now she's going to make cheese."

After my parents visited, they said it reminded them of how things were "back in the day." A niece and nephew who visited said it was like *Little House on the Prairie*. I was happy for the visits, proud to show off my new town and my wilderness independence.

For all the church rules I may have broken in the years after leaving home, I had never had my hair cut beyond a minimal trim. Mother may have thought it was because I was following the biblical injunction in Corinthians that a "woman's hair is a glory to her head." I didn't correct her, but for me over the years it had more to do with the women I admired who had long hair, women like Joan Baez, Judy Collins, and Joni Mitchell. My long, naturally curly hair was not easy to manage. I applied hair gel and wrapped it around giant rollers. It was obvious my hair did not want to be straight. I pulled it back into ponytails or flips or twists, but I did not have it cut until I got to Helvetia.

The well went dry frequently during the first months I was there, and I decided to get my hair cut to a length easier to care for . . . my first real haircut. I was relieved to free my curls to do what they wanted. When I visited home late that fall, Mother was shocked and disappointed when she saw my hair. Years later, I would see she had written in her diary that day: "Mary Alice got her hair cut, so the world has lost some of its joy." I had not experienced it that way at all.

One afternoon I was surprised when a group of Mennonites showed up unannounced at my door. They were part of a community a few hours away and had heard through some Mennonite grapevine that I had moved to Helvetia. They wanted to invite me to come worship with them. Their visit felt odd; I didn't know any of them. Although it may have been a welcoming gesture, the idea that I would drive that far to be with them, just because they were Mennonites, felt very strange to me.

I often went to the little church right there in town. It was Presbyterian, but it might have been anything. It was a place where people in town gathered. The mostly older congregation preferred the traditional, familiar hymns, which I knew well, and I was surprised by how comforting it felt to sing them. The minister, who had moved to Helvetia after retiring from a more demanding assignment, was a gentle man, given to sermons filled with metaphors from nature and references to things he had read. It was a spiritual context that resonated with me. His sermons included no talk of hellfire or latter days, no urgent messages about the need to be born again. The prayer requests were news updates, reports on who was sick, visiting children, or facing challenging life decisions.

When winter came, the visits from family and friends slowed and then stopped. Townspeople there told me "snow and solitude are what winter here is about." It seemed that no one in Helvetia expected any of the businesses would be up and running until spring, but there was a lot to do to get ready, and I tackled the tasks one at a time. Handymen responded slowly to my requests to check leaky roofs or bad water pipes. There was no point in being impatient—they'd get to it when they could. Little by little I worked my way down the list of repair and cleaning needs, but I had a lot of time for myself. Every two weeks, if travel permitted, the bookmobile came through and parked across the street from the store. I checked out stacks of books and spent hours reading. I found myself especially drawn to books with "journal" or "diary" or "journey" in their titles. I read books by Hal Borland, Anaïs Nin, Madeline L'Engle, Gladys Taber, and Doris Schwerin, and I kept a journal of quotes from my reading.

Sitting at my desk by the living room window and watching the snow pile up in the backyard, I worked on the novel I had always planned to write. A friend and I had been talking about our books for years, discussing our ideas for plots and characters as we shared drinks and dinners. The book I had outlined to him was set in the suburbs, but when I sat down to write that winter, it had transplanted to the farm of my childhood, a texture far more vivid in my imagination, no matter how hard I had tried to move away from it.

As I sat and wrote in the snowy solitude, I had no problem getting in touch with the landscape details of my growing-up years, but I could only imagine them as a setting for a novel. I never dreamed the day would come when I no longer saw the need to veil my story in fiction.

I walked for miles that winter and taught myself to cross-country ski, exploring back roads and logging trails. I got to know the townspeople and listened to their stories. The snow stacked up higher and higher, and the icicles hanging from the rock ledges on the roadside towered over me.

The combination store and post office was the hub of the town, and showing up once a day was a way of taking attendance, making sure everyone was all right. Some of the elderly people didn't like walking to the store if it was snowy or icy, so I took them their mail when the weather was bad. I was happy to drop in and listen to their stories.

Pete lived two doors down from the store, and he always showed up, no matter the weather. When I ran into him, he'd mention he'd seen me cleaning at the restaurant or pruning the hedges in front of the Cheese Haus. He'd smile, as if bemused by my efforts to beat back the wilderness. I was never certain if he was being friendly or laughing at me, but it didn't matter.

In January, Pete told me the sap would soon be running, and he was sure I'd want to make maple syrup. I hadn't thought about it, but of course I wanted to make maple syrup. He said I could buy the taps to drill into the trees, but he knew I'd want to whittle my own from willow shoots, the way they used to do it. One day he brought me a handful of willow shoots he'd cut from his tree out back. He had brought his whittling knife and showed me how to shave off the edge of the shoot and hollow out the soft sapwood in the middle. I sat down beside him by the stove to try it myself. He said it would be a few weeks till the sap was up, but he'd tell me when it was time and show me where the sugar maples were. "Otherwise," he said, his blue eyes twinkling, "you'll be drilling into oak trees or telephone poles." I took the willow taps back to my house and put them in water to keep them moist until it was time to drill holes and tap them into the trees. "Can't let them dry out," Pete said, "or they'll crack, and the sap'll leak every place but in the bucket."

Pete pointed out the sugar maples and told me when the sap was running. He showed me how to drill holes and insert the taps. I waited for the sap to drip into the buckets, and it didn't take long. I collected it several times a day and boiled it down in a big copper kettle, trying to keep the fire going day and night. For all my efforts, the sap never turned into the rich maple syrup I imagined, but the experience gave me an understanding of the process and a new appreciation for the high cost of pure maple syrup.

That winter I spent a good deal of time with Mary, a gracious and generous town matriarch who had once run the store and post office and still lived in the attached house. She was always busy doing something when I stopped in, sewing or cooking or baking, but she still had time to talk to me, answer my questions, and teach me whatever skills she could. Many of the things she taught me were things Mother might have taught if I had taken the time to learn them. Mother had taught me the art of quilting, but the quilts she made had ordered patchwork designs. When I mentioned to Mary I'd like to learn to make a crazy quilt, she pulled out her box of fabric scraps and showed me how to do it. I found the piecing easy, but it was more difficult to learn the fancy embroidery stitches used to embellish the seams. She taught me all the stitches she knew—the feather stitch, blanket stitch, cross stitch, wheat stitch, chicken foot stitch—and said I could probably make up some of my own.

One afternoon I stopped in to see her after I picked up my mail. She'd told me I could tap on the door that connected the store and her house. She offered me a cup of tea made from the mint she'd dried, and we sat at her kitchen table. "If I wanted to know about making cheese," I said, "who could I talk to?"

"Anything about cheese," Mary said, "you need to go see the Balli girls. They've always made the best cheese around. Those three been farming on their own ever since their brother died, and that was years ago."

"You have their phone number?"

Mary laughed. "Oh, they don't have a phone."

She wrote out directions. "When you look at these, you're gonna think it's a ways, but it's really not that far. "

"Shouldn't I make an appointment?"

"No. They're used to people coming by. They sell cheese. Spring is when they start making it again. In a few weeks, they should have some ready."

The days grew longer. Snow on the top of the mountains melted, and water trickling down the hills turned into rushing streams. The icicles on the side of the roads grew shorter and shorter, and finally disappeared; the stream that ran in front of my cottage turned into a river.

It was a sunny spring day when I headed out to find the Balli girls. I unfolded Mary's directions and spread them out on the passenger seat. Beyond Pickens and Turkey Bone I turned onto unpaved back roads. I steered to straddle muddy ruts and finally found the farm. A peeling handmade sign hanging on the fence read "Balli."

I waited in the car until a woman came out on the porch and calmed the barking German shepherd. She waved, signaling for me to come on in. I was nervous, dropping in on people I had never met, and I wasn't sure about the dog.

I went up to the door, and the woman introduced herself as Freda. She invited me inside, where two older women worked at a patchwork quilt stretched on a frame. It was a simple nine-patch. The Balli girls at the quilt barely looked at me when they said hello. All three of the women wore knit slacks and heavy sweaters, even though it was warm from the woodstove in the kitchen. Their hair was gray, and they had simple, short haircuts, all similar. It looked as if they might have on occasion taken turns cutting each other's hair. The Balli girls looked sturdy enough, but I was surprised they were still doing farm work on their own. A small black-and-white television sat on a shelf in the corner across from where they were quilting. They were watching a soap opera, and, with the poor reception, all the actors had shimmering shadows.

I glanced around the room at the furniture, which in another context might have been considered antique. In that place it just felt like furniture.

"How can we help you today?" Freda said.

"I wondered if you have any cheese on hand. Mary told me you sometimes sell it."

"We sure do. Started up making it again last month. First ones are getting ready. Come down to the basement with me and pick one out."

I followed Freda down the steep basement stairs. She pulled the cord to turn on the light, a single bulb suspended from the rafter. A series of screened shelves hung from the ceiling.

"The ones at the end are the oldest," she said, pointing to the bottom shelf. The blocks of cheese on the shelves were almost as big as loaves of bread, more cheese than I would usually eat in a year, but Freda didn't offer to divide it, so I didn't ask. I took the whole block, the oldest one she had. I knew that with cheese, age was a good thing.

We went back upstairs, talked a bit about the weather, about when the ramps would be ready. Ramps were wild onions that grew in the woods in the area, and folks were excited about the coming ramp season. They were already making plans for the annual Ramp Festival and looking for volunteers to help. I didn't know what ramps looked like or what to do with them, but I said I'd help clean them if someone showed me how to do it.

After I paid for my cheese, and I could think of nothing to do but leave, I asked, "So how do you make your cheese?"

With scarcely a pause, Freda said, "All you do is take some milk, heat it up, and add your rennet. After that it's time and patience. There's no hurrying cheese."

The instructions weren't a lot to go on, but clearly it was all I was going to get. For the Balli girls, it was the time of day for quilting and soap operas. I thanked them and left, no more certain how to make cheese than I was before I stopped by.

I drove slowly back to town. When I got home, I cut open the block of cheese and tasted it. The Balli girls' cheese was good, with a mild taste, like a Muenster. I wrapped a piece of it in plastic wrap and took it up to Mary. She was quilting.

"Did you learn to make cheese?" she asked.

"All you do is heat up some milk. The way I heard it, that's pretty much all there is to it."

Mary laughed. "Guess those Ballis don't want to give away their secrets."

Melvin, a dairy farmer who lived up on the ridge, heard I might be starting up the cheesemaking operation. I ran into him at the store one day, and he said he'd be glad to sell me milk. He could spare a couple of cans every other day, and he'd deliver it. He thought his wife, Gladys, would be willing to come down and show me how to make cheese. He told me she sometimes made it at home for the family, had been doing it for years. He thought hers was every bit as good as the Balli's.

Cheesemaking was one of the skills the early settlers to Helvetia had brought with them from their Swiss mountain homes. I was sure more people than Gladys and the Ballis could still make cheese, but I could find no one eager to take on the job, so I decided to get things going on my own. I called Gladys, and we chose a day to have her come down. She was clear with me that she had time to teach me, but she had no interest in being the regular cheesemaker.

There were fresh cobwebs in the Cheese Haus where I had cleaned months before. I undertook a thorough cleaning, scrubbing the shelves and floor, polishing the copper kettle to a brilliant shine with vinegar and salt, and soaking the dried-out wooden utensils.

One morning Melvin dropped off Gladys and two cans of milk. She was a patient teacher, guiding me through the steps of cheesemaking. She answered my questions, and I took careful notes. First we heated the milk slowly in the big copper kettle until it reached ninety degrees. It took a long time to heat so much milk, and Gladys was insistent we not turn the burner up.

"You've got to keep that burner on low," Gladys said. "If you scorch the milk, the cheese is ruined."

When the milk was warm, we stirred in the dissolved rennet and left it to set. It was a slow process, and Gladys and I ran out of things to talk about. While the milk cooled and the curd set, Gladys walked up the street to see her mother-in-law. I pulled weeds from the flower beds outside the Cheese Haus.

When we both got back, we removed the cover from the copper kettle. The watery whey was already separating from the gelled curd.

"What is rennet?" I asked Gladys when I saw the effect it had on the milk.

"It's what separates the curds from the whey," she said.

Only years later, when I had the chance to research it, did I learn that rennet was an enzyme derived from the lining of a cow's stomach, and some think the discovery of cheese may well have been a lucky accident. It seems a shepherd thousands of years ago may have poured milk into a bladder made from a cow's stomach. After wandering about for a time, he discovered that the sloshing milk had separated into curds and whey.

Gladys showed me how to cut the curds with the long wooden knife, and then it was time to heat it slowly again, this time to 120 degrees. We cooled it, stirring constantly to separate the curds and whey, rolling up our sleeves and mixing it with our hands, feeling for the bigger curds and gently breaking them. We drained off the whey, dipped out the curds, and pressed them into the wooden molds lined with muslin, weighing them down with bricks and leaving them to drain.

That first day, when Gladys noticed the front of my shirt was wet from splashing milk and whey, she said, "You'll probably want to get an apron, or you'll splash milk all over yourself." On my next trip to town, I found a denim apron at the hardware store. I appliquéd a red gingham heart onto the bib and embroidered vines in red thread. Gladys was right. The apron helped a lot.

In a couple of days the cheeses were dry enough to remove from the molds. Then it was all about turning and rubbing and aging, moving the blocks of cheese down the wooden shelves to make way for more, and waiting.

The restaurant opened in late May, on weekends at first, and then every day but Monday, when I made the long drive to Elkins for supplies. The woman who had cooked when the restaurant opened some years earlier was happy to come back, glad to be able to earn money to supplement her husband's disability benefits. She already knew the health inspector's rules and had her hairnets and refrigerator thermometers in place. Local high school and college students applied to be waitresses. I filled in by waiting tables, cooking, or washing dishes. On the mornings I made cheese, while the curd was setting, I went out into the woods or fields to pick fresh wildflowers to put in vases on the tables. We had a limited menu and only ten tables, but there was a steady flow of customers all summer. They stopped at the restaurant on their way to camp at one of the area's state parks or to drive over the mountains for a day trip from the nearest towns. Local people ate at the restaurant for special occasions. The grilled cheese sandwiches on homemade bread with sides of home fries and warm applesauce blended with horseradish was one of the most popular dishes. No matter what the dish, we always served a piece of Helvetia cheese, sometimes with a slice of fruit, berries, or fresh vegetables, whatever was available. I had tried putting wildflowers on the plates with the cheese, but the cook was insistent that if you couldn't eat it, it did not belong on a plate. She might have allowed buttonweeds, but I never saw them growing in the West Virginia mountains.

Through the summer, cheesemaking went on with meditative regularity. During that time I often woke to milk cans clanging, a sound familiar from my childhood. I made cheese every other day, blocks of it. Sometimes Gladys filled in, and I trained one of the summer workers to help out. When word got out we had cheese available, we had no problem selling it.

During the months I tended my cheeses, the flavor changed with the season as Melvin's cows changed their diet. It may have been something in the milk or the humidity of dog days creeping into the curing room. Whatever it was, for a few weeks the cheese bacteria grew in uncontrollable and unpredictable ways. Blocks of cheese were bloated and misshapen, with oozing air pockets inside. I asked Gladys about it, and she tried to reassure me, saying it happened sometimes. I doubted it ever happened to the Balli girls. One evening at dusk I loaded the spoiled cheeses into my car, drove up beyond the cemetery, and flung them from the side of the road, over the rhododendrons and into the darkening woods.

A few weeks later, feeling guilty, I hiked down into the woods to look for the cheeses I feared might still be there littering the forest. I walked back and forth where I was sure I had thrown them and couldn't find a trace. I was relieved they were gone. It was as if the bad cheeses had never happened.

During that first year I learned to weave baskets from honeysuckle vines. I made wine from dandelion blossoms, blackberries, and elderberries. I tried unsuccessfully to make beer from hops that grew behind the restaurant, sealing the bottles too quickly and causing a chain-reaction explosion up and down the basement stairs, glass shards everywhere, and beer dripping from the rafters. I beat back the kudzu and multiflora rose ever-encroaching on the buildings. Some days it felt to me as if I was living the life of a pioneer woman, a way of life far more primitive than that of the "farmer's wife" I had once sworn I'd never be.

At the end of my year's leave, I could not imagine returning to the Main Line and chose instead to stay in Helvetia for a second year. I resigned from my teaching position and gave up my apartment. I settled in for another winter and opened the restaurant and Cheese Haus again in the spring.

Now, so many years later, I'm still not sure I understand all of what my Helvetia interlude was about. I approached the time with no Thoreau-like intention to go to the woods "because I wished to live deliberately." To say it was about needing a break feels too simple, although my initial intent was probably not very different from what Mother felt when she was hoeing corn in the hot summer sun and went to the shade under the tree at the end of the row for what she called "a breather." It was a breather, and it did give me time and space to live more deliberately, but it was more than that. I had thought the experience would be a brief detour, but I had gone too far on the "road less traveled" to find my way back, even if I had wanted to.

No other two years changed the course of my life quite so dramatically. The experience and the quiet solitude it afforded helped me tap into a space deep inside I hadn't known was there. I had been so busy trying to become someone I wasn't that I did not give myself time and space to discover who I was. I was in such a hurry to reject my upbringing that I didn't allow for the possibility of not rejecting all of it. In my frenzy to fit in new experiences, I hadn't realized I also needed to slow down and discover the worth of experiences I'd already had. Being authentic was not something I had given much thought before I moved to the mountains.

I can imagine there may have been new conversations among friends and family who wondered what happened to my ambition after my time in Helvetia. Although my subsequent career in human services involved working with adolescents and education, I never returned to the classroom. My ambitions in some ways became much more modest. Slowly,

I came to realize that for me the true art of a life is in the sheer living of it, learning what I can from the people and experiences I encounter each day, and giving back however I can along the way.

I began to acknowledge the value of Mother's practical philosophy of each day, "just doing what needs to be done" and "what you don't get done one day, leave for another." Although I was a person very different from her, I gradually came to respect her simple philosophy and realized that in some ways we were more similar than I had previously thought.

In that place, I could reclaim the landscape of my childhood. In my hurry to get away, I had not noticed the beauty in simplicity, had not acknowledged the security of belonging to something bigger than myself. In my zeal to pull up roots, like on that long-ago day when I made vegetable soup, I realized I may have left some vegetables in the ground, like the biggest of the potatoes. As Mother told me, the big ones are those that grow deep, and it sometimes takes longer to get to them.

I have no illusions that I made lasting changes in Helvetia, the place that changed my life's direction. I hope some of the cedars I replanted next to the Cheese Haus have taken hold. And I hope the rhododendrons I moved from up on the ridge and planted behind the restaurant, probably violating a state law, have grown into the dramatic bank of color I had envisioned. Most of the people I knew when I lived in Helvetia are now gone—Mary, Pete, the Balli girls, and so many others. I see their obituaries in the church newsletter I receive a couple of times a year. I know I could not have stayed there. The businesses scarcely generated enough income to cover expenses, and I had used up most of my savings. In truth, I wanted more. Yet I don't regret any of my time and experiences there. All of it taught me valuable lessons in watching and waiting—for the icicles to melt, for the curds to separate from the whey, for the cheese to age, for the maple sap to run—for all those things that cannot be hurried.

Among those things that could not be hurried was the realization that, for all those years I assumed the right man would one day come along, I was attracted to another woman. At first I was willing to admit it only to myself; admitting it to anyone else was out of the question. It had to be a fluke. Surely it did not make me one of "those people."

For me, coming to terms with being a lesbian was a dawning as gradual as morning's first light. There were no lightning bolts, no epiphanies, no before-and-after moment. It was a slow peeling away of layers until I had to accept the unavoidable truth that what I was feeling was more than a stage I was passing through, that, no matter how hard I might try to deny it, it was my truth. I was embarrassed that I had been clueless for so long that, for all my attempts to be worldly wise, I had been naive. It was both freeing and frightening coming to terms with this new reality. And there was joy in knowing that I could love and be loved.

As I got to know more lesbians and heard their stories, I initially latched onto the stories from women who talked about having crushes on teenage girlfriends or being attracted to women teachers. Since none of those felt like my story, I was reassured for a time that maybe I wasn't a real lesbian. There were many other stories, some more similar to mine, but those I paid less attention to, since they did not support my dubious thesis.

Being new to the lesbian experience, I had no idea of the games I would learn to play. I didn't yet know I would come to participate in the foolish charade of pretending I was single and still looking for the perfect guy, or acting as if long-term partners were casual roommates. For all my efforts over the years to fit in, I feared my new truth could put me at odds with family and society at large in ways I could not have imagined. I didn't want to risk losing my job or connections to friends and family. Even if I had no reason to believe those things would happen for me, I had heard enough stories to know it was a possibility. For far too long, I was willing to behave as if my truth was something to hide, certainly not to celebrate.

Although I came away from my West Virginia respite feeling in most ways more aware and in touch with what was important to me, it would take years before I became totally honest with myself, let alone the people in my world, about all of who I was.

# The Coming-Out Letters

By the time I was in my fifties, years after my time in Helvetia, I had become more open and honest with friends, coworkers, and some family members about being a lesbian. Some of them may have already known, not because I told them but because they figured out the obvious. But I was certainly not out to my parents. My mother had died not knowing, and my father was in his mid-nineties. I saw no need to change the comfortable, if somewhat dishonest, status quo that had been established.

The first letter was not mine, although my brother Charles and I had spent so much time talking about it that I felt some ownership. My partner and I had gone to San Francisco to visit Charles for the Thanksgiving holiday. We had read and reread the letter he was planning to send Daddy, changing a word here and there, rearranging sentences. I suggested he replace "gay" with "homosexual," the word Daddy was more likely to have heard, usually in the same sentence with "abomination," from the pulpit of the Mennonite Church he and my mother had attended for decades.

I had heard those words myself when I attended my parents' church years before. The "abomination of homosexuality" was the theme of the sermon, and the minister was passionate on the topic, speaking of it with such zeal, it was as if he had singlehandedly discovered a new sin.

I was supportive of Charles, respected his courage, and was flattered that he valued my opinion about something so important, but I didn't fully understand his need to write the letter.

"You really think Daddy needs to know? You think this is going to help him?" I said.

"It's not for him," Charles said. "I'm doing this for me. I'm almost sixty years old, and he still thinks I'll get married if I find the right woman.

"It's not like he's rejected you or anything. He thinks the sun rises and sets on his doctor sons."

"I don't know what he'll do with this, but I need him to know who I am."

"He's just obsessed about that letter," I told my partner later.

"Sounds like it's important to him for your father to know," she said.

"I think Daddy's doing the best he can. He never went beyond eighth grade, and he's been a farmer his whole life. His world's pretty narrow. He's ninety-five years old. Something like this, no telling how he might take it."

"You might be surprised," she said.

The next morning, after breakfast, Charles asked if I wanted to walk with him to the mailbox. The sun was glistening off the buildings on the San Francisco skyline against a brilliant blue sky. We walked to Fillmore, and I watched my brother drop his letter in the slot.

"There it goes," he said.

"No taking it back now," I said.

We took the long way home, through Alamo Square Park, the iconic Painted Ladies lined up in the morning light.

"I wonder who'll be the first to visit him after he gets the letter, who'll get to hear about it first and process it with him," Charles said.

Two of my eight brothers who lived near the nursing home in Pennsylvania checked in on him every week. Abe was a psychiatrist; Ike, a retired farmer and Mennonite deacon.

"I know Abe goes every Wednesday afternoon," I said, "and I think Ike goes on Friday."

"I doubt it will get there by Wednesday," Charles said.

My partner and I flew back home to Virginia, and the busyness of catching up at work and getting ready for the holidays distracted me from thinking too much about the letter or wondering when the news would hit the family grapevine. It didn't take long before the reports started trickling in, each tidbit so remarkable I began to keep a record. My father showed the letter to my brother Ike first.

"Did you know this?" Daddy was reported to have asked him.

"Everyone pretty much knows it."

"Well, I sure didn't," Daddy said. "Had no idea."

By the following Wednesday, when Abe visited, my father had some questions.

"How does this happen?" he asked.

"It seems that some people are just born that way," Abe said.

"Are a lot of them born that way?"

"Some people say about one in ten, but there's no telling."

"Well, if it's how people are born, it sure doesn't seem like something that should tear families apart."

That proclamation rippled up and down the family grapevine and was so remarkable, it should have reverberated down the halls of Fair Haven Nursing Home, past the nurse's station, across the fields, echoing off the barns and silos, the plain brick Mennonite churches.

After Daddy received and processed the letter from Charles, he seemed to spend a good deal of time in his sunny room contemplating this new reality. The one-in-ten theory seemed to stick with him, and, from his vantage point overlooking the nursing home entrance, he may have counted off visitors, wondering. He talked to visiting family members about unmarried relatives, neighbors, wondering.

When my brother Sanford visited, Daddy said, "You know, I've been thinking about Eli." Eli was an Amish neighbor. "All those years he worked that farm by himself. I remember when he was younger, he dated girls, but it just didn't seem to work out for him. I wonder if that was the story with Eli. It makes me feel bad that he never found someone."

And then the questions started about me.

"It makes me wonder about Mary Alice," Daddy said. "What about her?"

"I guess you should ask her," Sanford said, but of course Daddy wasn't going to. It wasn't the sort of thing we talked about.

When Sanford told me about the conversation, I knew it was time to clear things up, to let my father know that I was part of the one-in-ten. I could have dispatched a sibling to deliver my news. I could have shouted it to my hearing-impaired father over the phone or on my next visit. A letter seemed like the most reliable way to communicate.

After Charles's courageous letter, I knew mine would be anticlimactic, not only because his came first but also because I was a daughter, and, in our family, especially from my father's point of view, nothing about being a daughter had the same import as it would have from a son. So I wrote my letter and sent it, but during subsequent visits, the subject never came up. Daddy was as welcoming to my partner and me as he had always been. I considered asking him about the letter, but I never did.

My primary relationship had always been with Mother. It was only after her death that I had occasion to have telephone conversations with my father, or one-on-one connections when I visited. It was always Mother I'd talk to on visits or on the phone. It was she who would write letters and birthday notes. I had never considered my father a particularly wise man, so the gentle wisdom in his response to the Coming-Out letter from Charles surprised and delighted me. I liked to believe he felt the same way about my letter.

If Mother had still been alive, I think any follow-up conversation would have been outsourced to her. They had lived in the nursing home together for a couple of years before she died at the age of ninety-five, just a few weeks after they celebrated their seventy-fourth wedding anniversary.

For years after she died, Daddy glanced toward her chair when he needed to tell her something or ask her opinion, and I'm sure he would have liked to know what she thought of the letters. I can only hope she would have been as understanding as my father was, but I'll never know.

The nursing home where my parents lived was run by conservative Mennonites and was consistently recognized for its cleanliness and the quality of its care. Many of the staff members considered their work a religious calling. A steady stream of volunteers cleaned the residents' eyeglasses, shined their shoes, massaged their feet, and filled the halls and chapels with music.

Daddy ate all his meals in the dining room, but he insisted on having a full-size refrigerator in his room so he had space in the freezer to store his Turkey Hill Black Cherry Ice Cream, which my brothers made sure he always had on hand. He kept the bowls and spoons in the refrigerator, along with pretzel sticks and pink mints for visiting children. He served himself a snack each evening.

As one of only a handful of men in the nursing home, he seemed to think he was much sought after by the widows. He made it clear he had no intention of remarrying, but he did invite some of them over for a bowl of ice cream now and then. His vision of heaven was one that would reunite him with his beloved wife, and he looked forward to that . . . but first he wanted to live to be one hundred or at least exceed the life span of his older brother, who had died just short of ninety-nine.

In time, my father's focus on who was or wasn't gay abated. The reality blended into the landscape of carefully tended farms stretching as far as he could see from his window. Sometimes I liked to imagine him sitting in the sunroom with the three other men in his wing at the nursing home—all of them hard of hearing—and hear him shouting, "And I have two children who are gay. What do you make of that?" Perhaps I wanted him to be more courageous than I had been.

Daddy died a week short of his one hundredth birthday. I think it gave him peace knowing that all twelve of his children found someone with whom to share their lives. If he's with my mother in heaven, I hope he's brought her up-to-date on family news. If he's run into Eli, his Amish neighbor, I expect he told him how sorry he was that Eli had to work the farm by himself all those years.

A few years ago, many of the Mennonite churches in Lancaster County, including the church where my parents were members, voted to split from Mennonite Church USA over that organization's decision to allow gay members. The only thing as important as church to my parents was family, and I'm glad they did not live to see this time when they might need to make a choice. Would church or family win? Would Daddy speak up against his church to say "It's not the sort of thing to tear families apart?"

After the Supreme Court made same-sex marriage legal, my long-time partner and I chose to be married. We had been together for eighteen years. I don't know what my parents would have made of that, but I wish they could have been at the wedding.

# EPILOGUE

# Elegy to the Farm
# Where I Grew Up

Now, when I return to the landscape of my growing-up years and drive by the farm where I grew up, I do not turn in the lane once shaded by a canopy of catalpa trees. I do not drive by the rock garden where the "Slow, Children at Play" sign that Grace painted once stood among the hostas. It could as easily have said, "Slow, Children at Work."

From the road I can see the wash house where we boiled lye soap in the big iron kettle. We took turns stirring, careful not to splash, before Mother grabbed the big iron ladle from its hook and dipped the hot liquid into the soap pans to harden. When we butchered hogs, the air in the wash house was filled with smoke and the smell of rendered lard.

The house where I grew up is gone, burned to the ground a few years after the new owners moved in. The cook stove, Mother told me, overheated as the Amish farmer's wife was roasting turkeys. In three days they cleared the rubble, and friends and neighbors helped them build a new house. It looks nothing like the house where I grew up.

How could the kitchen be gone, the space that held so much? The long table, all those meals together, homework in the evening, and on Sunday, board games. All the canning and freezing, baking and boiling. The kitchen . . . the hub of it all.

The bedroom I shared with Nancy, the room overlooking the garden, is gone. Also, of course, the sweet potato barrel that stood in the corner, because our room stayed cold in winter. In the new house, with windows that may not rattle in the wind, the bedroom may be too warm for storing sweet potatoes.

The big front bedroom, my parents' room, gone. Most of us were born there, the family doctor called out in the night, early morning, evening. For me, it was early morning. Thousands of prayers silently prayed as my parents knelt beside the sagging bed. The room, my parents, all ashes now. I do not know what happened to the prayers.

And the egg room in the basement, where Nancy and I spent hours cleaning and grading eggs: Did the house come crashing in on it as it burned? Did it tear off the drain pipe where I taped poems and vocabulary words and lists of state capitols to memorize as I cleaned and graded eggs? Did the Amish farmer's wife, like my mother, use the shelves along the wall to store canned goods? Were the jars knocked off the shelves and broken, pickles and beets floating in the applesauce, strawberry jam oozing into chow-chow?

Beyond the new house, beyond the wash house, the corn crib has been turned into a stable for mules; the stripping room next to the cow stable is now used for storing harnesses. Before I was born, my father, brothers, and uncles stripped tobacco in that space, pulling it down from the scaffolding in the barn lathe by lathe, pulling off the leaves to bale and sell. When I was a child, we used the room, still smelling faintly of tobacco, to sort and bag potatoes. Now it may smell of harness leather. The new owners wouldn't know to call it the stripping room.

In the front yard three evergreens grow side by side where the big weeping willow once stood. It came down in Hurricane Hazel and was sawed up and carried away. After that, Mother couldn't make willow whistles anymore. I thought she might have saved some branches, the straight ones with the buds far apart, kept them moist, but there was too much work to do. I could never make a sound with those willow whistles, and Mother said, "When you're older, you'll be able to blow harder," but by then the tree was gone.

And what remains is memory and story.

# Acknowledgments

So many people have played a part in this book's creation, and a complete list would be far too long, but here are a few thanks.

I acknowledge, with gratitude, my parents, especially my mother, who patiently endured my questions and challenges, even when they must have grown tedious; and my siblings, who shared in this journey, all in their own way, and who might understandably have reservations about having a memoir writer in the family. I know their experiences may have been different from mine, and each of them, no doubt, has a different version of the story. And I am deeply appreciative of my many nieces and nephews for their friendships and interest in my writing.

I am indebted to the many teachers I have worked with over the years at the International Women's Writing Guild Summer Conference. I acknowledge those who have encouraged me to excavate my life, insisting I have a story worth telling and the responsibility to tell it: Eunice Scarfe, Susan Tiberghien, Maureen Murdock, Pat Carr, Judy Huge, Jan Phillips, June Gould, Lisa Dale Norton. And I am grateful for the sustaining friendships forged in that nurturing space, especially that of Ruth Steinberg and Barbara Haber, whose support over the years has been unwavering.

I offer special thanks to Sharon Harrigan and Jay Varner, nonfiction teachers at WriterHouse in Charlottesville, who helped me continue the excavation of my memory and give form and meaning to the fragments I discovered. When I submitted a proposal to be part of Sharon Harrigan's inaugural memoir class, including as a writing sample a collection of random pieces in various stages of development, she had faith that I could shape the material into a memoir. This book might not have happened without her encouragement and help in creating a meaningful and cohesive vessel to contain these shards of memory.

My gratitude to the students I have studied with, whose scribbled margin notes have helped make my work better. It has been a luxury to have had those early readers. I would particularly like to thank Lisa Ellison, Carole Duff, and Kristin Sancken for their careful reading, thoughtful critiques, and belief in this project.

I am grateful to the Virginia Center for the Creative Arts for providing fellowships that offered the luxury of uninterrupted time and space to write, and to Bama Works, who supported those fellowships.

I appreciate the editors who have encouraged me by publishing my work, particularly Daniel Jones, Michael King, Tracy Crow, Terry Kennedy, Jason Howard, Susan Shafarzek, and Peter Stitt. And I am grateful for all the support from the staff of the University of Wisconsin Press— Dennis Lloyd, Nathan MacBrien, Holly McArthur, Sheila McMahon, Jennifer Conn, Alison Shay—whose vision and efforts made this book possible.

Thanks to my early beta readers who so generously offered their time to read the manuscript: Lorna Facteau, Ruth Steinberg, Joyce Jacobson, Sarah Cohn, Ella Clemens, Conrad Clemens. And to my family readers: Rhoda, Charles, Sanford, and Nancy.

And to my wife, Terry, simple gratitude does not seem adequate for all you have done to encourage me at every stage of the journey to bring this book to life, reading more rough drafts than anyone should be subjected to. And you have done more to open my heart to love and beauty than you will ever know.

Grateful acknowledgment is made for the first publication of some of the chapters, some in slightly different form: "Yearnings" (*Hippocampus*, 2019); "Wrestling with Peace" (*Streetlight*, 2018); "On Foot-Washing Sunday" (*DreamSeeker*, 2008); "Zeit und Raum" (*Gettysburg Review*, 2014); "The Coming-Out Letters," published as "Dear Dad, We've Been Gay for a Very Long Time" (*New York Times* [Modern Love], 2016; "Elegy to the Farm Where I Grew Up" (*The Common*, 2019).

# Living Out

Gay and Lesbian Autobiographies
David Bergman, Joan Larkin, and Raphael Kadushin,
*Founding Editors*

*Eminent Maricones: Arenas, Lorca, Puig, and Me*
Jaime Manrique

*1001 Beds: Performances, Essays, and Travels*
Tim Miller

*Body Blows: Six Performances*
Tim Miller

*Cleopatra's Wedding Present: Travels through Syria*
Robert Tewdwr Moss

*Good Night, Beloved Comrade: The Letters of Denton Welch to Eric Oliver*
Edited and with an introduction by Daniel J. Murtaugh

*Taboo*
Boyer Rickel

*Men I've Never Been*
Michael Sadowski

*Secret Places: My Life in New York and New Guinea*
Tobias Schneebaum

*Wild Man*
Tobias Schneebaum

*Sex Talks to Girls: A Memoir*
Maureen Seaton

*Treehab: Tales from My Natural, Wild Life*
Bob Smith

*The Change: My Great American, Postindustrial, Midlife Crisis Tour*
Lori Soderlind

*Outbound: Finding a Man, Sailing an Ocean*
William Storandt

*Given Up for You: A Memoir of Love, Belonging, and Belief*
Erin O. White